Studies in the Psychology of Music
Volume V

# A Three-Year Longitudinal Predictive Validity Study of the Musical Aptitude Profile

## EDWIN GORDON

UNIVERSITY OF IOWA PRESS Ψ IOWA CITY

# ACKNOWLEDGMENTS

The writer is grateful for the assistance received from many persons in the designing, development, and the completion of this study. The Iowa Testing Programs under the auspices of the College of Education of The University of Iowa generously provided research grants. The National Association of Band Instrument Manufacturers made a gift of many musical instruments to The University of Iowa. Members of the Research Committee of the College of Education and individuals associated with the Measurement Research Center have unselfishly given time and advice. And, of course, without the important services and cooperation of the school music teachers and their administrators, the study would not have been completed.

Above all, the writer is most grateful to two persons for their invaluable guidance and assistance—Professor Paul J. Blommers and Dr. James Neilson.

Edwin Gordon
Iowa City, Iowa
January, 1967

iii

# TABLE OF CONTENTS

# LIST OF TABLES

# INTRODUCTION

The Musical Aptitude Profile was developed at The University of Iowa over a period of eight years of systematic research centering on the description and measurement of musical aptitude. During the latter part of this developmental period, a three-year longitudinal study of the validity of the Musical Aptitude Profile as a predictor of student achievement in instrumental music was begun. At the time of publication of the Musical Aptitude Profile in 1965, only the first-year results of this three-year study were available. Preliminary findings based on these first-year results were reported in the test Manual[1]. The primary purpose of this monograph is to provide a complete and final report of the findings of the three-year[2] study. In addition, a discussion of the effects of practice and training on Musical Aptitude Profile test scores and the relationship of environmental factors to the test scores follows the main report.

---

[1]Edwin Gordon, *Musical Aptitude Profile Manual* (Boston: Houghton Mifflin Company, 1965), p. 68-73.

[2] The three academic years beginning in the fall of 1963 and ending in the spring of 1966.

# DESCRIPTION OF THE MUSICAL APTITUDE PROFILE

The Musical Aptitude Profile was designed to provide objective information which could be used in conjunction with teachers' subjective judgments to evaluate the musical aptitudes of students enrolled in the upper elementary and secondary school grades. Such evaluations may be used for the following purposes:

1. To identify musically talented students who can profit most from and contribute most to school music activities.
2. To adapt music methods and materials to the individual needs and abilities of students by compensating for their specific musical weaknesses and by enhancing their specific musical strengths.
3. To aid in the formulation of educational plans in music.
4. To compare the collective musical aptitudes of groups of students.
5. To apprise parents of the musical aptitudes of their children.

The basic facets of musical ability measured by the Musical Aptitude Profile may be classified into three main divisions: Tonal Imagery, Rhythm Imagery, and Musical Sensitivity. There is an unequivocally correct or best answer to the items of the tests of the first two divisions. Consequently, it will be convenient to refer to these tests as nonpreference tests. The tests in the third division, on the other hand, are intended as measures of musical taste. These tests, which are keyed in conformance with the consensus of both students and professionals, will be referred to as preference tests. Two separate tests or subtests are provided for each of the nonpreference divisions. They are Melody and Harmony for the Tonal Imagery division, and Tempo and Meter for the Rhythm Imagery division. The preference test division, Musical Sensitivity, involves three separate tests or subtests, namely, Phrasing, Balance, and Style. Thus, in addition to providing for diagnostic appraisal of specific aspects of tonal and rhythmic aptitudes, the test battery also provides an appraisal of appreciation for musical expression and, indirectly, musical creativity.

The complete battery of seven tests, including practice exercises and directions, is recorded on magnetic tape. The test items consist of original

[1]

short selections composed for violin and cello and performed by professional artists.[1]

The tests are designed for all students in grades four through twelve. No prior formal music training is required as a prerequisite for taking the test. A normal general exposure to the sound of music and a seriousness of purpose are the only requirements.

The tests involve no questions dealing with historical or technical facts about music. Students are asked only to compare a musical selection or passage with a musical answer and, in the case of the nonpreference tests, to indicate on an answer sheet whether the two are alike or different or exactly the same or different. In the case of the preference tests, students are directed to indicate on the answer sheet which of two renditions of the same music represents a more tasteful musical performance. If the student is not sure of the answer to a given exercise, he is instructed to indicate that he is "in doubt" by marking the question-mark (?) column on the answer sheet and thus is not forced to make judgments on questions which he is incapable of answering.

In all, eleven test scores are obtained from the test battery: one score for each of the seven subtests; a total score for each of the three main divisions; and a composite score for the complete battery. Each of the four nonpreference subtests consists of forty exercises, and each of the preference subtests consists of thirty exercises, making a total of 250 exercises for the complete battery. The standard score scale for each test of the battery is based on a mean of fifty, a standard deviation of ten, and a range of approximately twenty through eighty.

The battery was standardized on a representative sample of public school students in grades four through twelve, selected on the basis of procedures developed for the Project Talent study which was conducted by the American Institute for Research in cooperation with the United States Office of Education.[2] Separate norms are provided for each grade from four through twelve. Special norms for students participating in school music organizations are also provided for three levels: elementary school (grades four, five, and six); junior high school (grades seven, eight, and nine); and senior high school (grades ten, eleven, and twelve).

During the eight-year developmental period, a great deal of experimen-

---

[1] Stuart Canin, violin; Charles Treger, violin; Paul Olefsky, cello. Mr. Canin was the first American to win the Paganini International Violin Competition in Genoa, Italy, in 1959. Mr. Treger was the first non-European to win the Henry Wieniawski International Violin Competition in Poznan, Poland, in 1962. Mr. Olefsky, among many other honors, has received the Michels Memorial Award.

[2] John Flanagan, et al. Project Talent (Pittsburgh: University of Pittsburgh Press, 1962).

[2]

tation centered on improving item difficulty and discrimination, and on improving the reliability characteristics of the various subtests without unduly increasing their length. The reliability coefficients of the tests are as high as those generally reported for academic and diagnostic achievement tests. Reliability coefficients differ somewhat from grade to grade and from test to test, but are generally in the .70's and .80's for individual subtests, in the .80's and .90's for main division composites, and in the .90's for the total battery. Specific reliabilities for each test for each grade, and the intercorrelation among the tests, are reported in the test Manual.[3]

A permanent cumulative music folder has been designed for use with the Musical Aptitude Profile. Test scores earned in the elementary, junior high, and senior high schools may be recorded in the folder along with other pertinent information. A student-parent report has also been designed for use with the test battery. The answer sheet is designed to provide for the option of electronic scoring and processing through the facilities of the Measurement Research Center, Iowa City, Iowa. This service includes a print-out of all eleven standard scores and their percentile ranks on pressure sensitive labels which greatly facilitates the transcription of this information to the student's folder and parent's report.

---

[3] Pp. 50, 56-57.

# PRELIMINARY EVIDENCE OF VALIDITY
# AND THE NEED FOR A LONGITUDINAL STUDY

The relationships between Musical Aptitude Profile scores and a variety of variables were investigated both during the eight-year test development period and in conjunction with the test standardization program. Correlations between aptitude test scores on the one hand and musical status, participation in music performance organizations, performance media, and sex on the other were obtained separately for grades four through twelve for all students in the standardization sample. Correlations between Musical Aptitude Profile test scores and achievement test scores and verbal and non-verbal intelligence test scores were obtained during the period in which the battery was developed. The effects of practice and training on Musical Aptitude Profile test scores and the diagnostic properties of the test battery were also investigated during the developmental period. The results of these studies are reported in detail in the test Manual.[1] It is, therefore, sufficient to note here that the effects of environmental factors and musical training on aptitude test performance appear to be relatively minimal and that the use of the profile as a diagnostic instrument is justified by the evidence available.

Preliminary evidence of the validity of the Musical Aptitude Profile in identifying musically talented students was obtained by correlating aptitude test scores with teacher ratings of students' musical ability and by correlating aptitude test scores with judges' evaluations of students' tape-recorded musical performances. These concurrent validity studies, reported in the test Manual, yielded reasonably high relationships.[2] However, it must be recognized that correlation coefficients of this type provide only minimal evidence of validity in the sense that while such coefficients are indeed a necessary consequence of validity, they may also arise in its absence. That is, a substantial concurrent relationship between aptitude

---

[1] Pp. 61-79.

[2] Pp. 58-61. Correlations between aptitude test composite scores and teachers' estimates of musical aptitude ranged from .64 to .97. Correlations with recorded performances were much lower (.12 to .55), perhaps owing somewhat to the fact that the groups exhibited a high degree of selectivity with regard to interest in, and talent for, musical performance as well as to the possible unreliability of such measures.

test scores and teachers' ratings or judges' evaluations of students' musical achievement describes only concomitant variation and not causation. Thus, it cannot be inferred that a student's musical aptitude scores are a primary result of his musical achievement or, conversely, that a student's musical achievement is a natural consequence of his demonstrated musical aptitude. All aptitude tests are, through necessity, to some degree achievement tests, just as all achievement test scores to some degree reflect aptitude, depending, of course, upon the extent to which the effect of achievement on performance has been successfully minimized or maximized in relation to the effect of aptitude.

A more satisfying method of evaluating the validity of an aptitude test (to predict the degree to which students can profit from and contribute to special music activities) involves (1) measuring musical aptitude prior to exposure to any substantial musical training; (2) the provision of a relatively uniform and extensive program of training; (3) the evaluation of musical accomplishment after training; and (4) a comparison of aptitude and accomplishment scores. Given such a longitudinal (over time) design, it would seem reasonable to infer that, in general, the aptitude scores ought to be relatively uninfluenced by the effects of formal training and consequent musical achievement. Correlations between the initial aptitude test scores with achievement test scores obtained after a substantially long period of training constitute much clearer evidence of the effectiveness of the aptitude test as a predictor of ability to profit from musical instruction. If it can be thus objectified (and not have to be necessarily inferred from concurrent relationships found with older musically trained students) that the Musical Aptitude Profile does function as an aptitude test, it can then be administered with confidence to students who have never received formal instruction in music for the purpose of assessing their musical aptitudes and for identifying those who can profit most from and contribute most to school music activities.

# THE THREE-YEAR LONGITUDINAL PREDICTIVE
# VALIDITY STUDY

*Design of the Study*

The three-year longitudinal predictive validity study of the Musical Aptitude Profile, a description of which is the subject of this report, was unique in the following respect. *All* enrolled students in selected fourth and fifth grade elementary school classrooms in Davenport, Cedar Falls, and Iowa City, Iowa, and in Racine, Wisconsin, were given a *minimum* of one group instrumental music lesson each week as a *curricular* activity, over a three-year period. (Students typically participated in additional music activities depending on their interest and achievement.) Thus, the subjects of this study were unselected and therefore constituted a heterogeneous group with respect to musical aptitude. Further, contrary to usual circumstances, the participating students had no previous formal music instruction other than what might be normally expected in a primary-grades general music program and, in rare instances, from lessons outside of school. As a consequence, validity of the test battery did not have to be inferred from data for a homogeneous group of musically select students.

Each participating student was provided with a new high-quality musical instrument, including flutes, clarinets, saxophones, trumpets, horns, cornets, trombones, and baritones.[1] The school systems provided instructional staff, typical methods books and music of the teachers' choosing, and other necessary materials.

Five criteria were followed in evaluating musical progress. These consisted of: adjudicator ratings of (1) melodic, rhythmic, and expressive aspects of tape-recorded performances of short etudes which the students prepared in advance with teacher help, (2) melodic, rhythmic, and ex-

---

[1] The instruments were furnished at no cost to either the school systems or the students through the generosity of the National Association of Band Instrument Manufacturers. Companies which either donated or consigned instruments to The University of Iowa for the purpose of conducting the study were: Artley, Incorporated, Elkhart, Indiana; Chicago Musical Instrument Company, Chicago, Illinois; C. G. Conn Limited, Elkhart, Indiana; Frank Holton Company, Elkhorn, Wisconsin; G. Leblanc Corporation, Kenosha, Wisconsin; and H. and A. Selmer, Incorporated, Elkhart, Indiana.

[6]

pressive aspects of tape-recorded performances of short etudes which the students prepared in advance but without teacher help, (3) melodic, rhythmic, and expressive aspects of tape-recorded performances of short etudes which the students sight read; (4) teacher ratings of each student's musical progress as compared with that of other students in the group; and (5) performance on an objective musical achievement test specifically designed to assess ability to identify musical notation associated with melodic, rhythmic, and harmonic passages heard on a tape-recording, and to assess knowledge of musical terms and signs.

The design of the study provided for the tape-recording of each student's performances of the three etudes twice during two adjacent weeks so as to permit an estimate of the stability (reliability) of student performance. Each student's recorded performances were independently rated by two judges, a member of the professorial staff of The University of Iowa School of Music and the writer. This not only made it possible to investigate inter-judge agreement (reliability), but also to achieve increased reliability through a pooling of the two ratings. To eliminate a possible source of rater bias, all tape-recorded performances were obtained by the individual music teachers and the performers were identified only by number on the recording. Moreover, the order in which the student performances were taped was changed at random for the second of the two weeks by the music teachers.

At the outset, 241 students were included in the study. These students comprised the total enrollment of eight classrooms in five different schools in four cities. Each of these students was given the Musical Aptitude Profile in September, 1963, *prior to the start of instrumental music instruction.* Of course, because of the nature of the study, neither the music teachers nor the adjudicators were apprised of students' pretraining aptitude test results until the study was completed. At the end of the three-year period, student musical achievement was evaluated and correlated with pretraining musical aptitude test scores. As ancillary parts of the study, the effects of environmental influences and practice and training on Musical Aptitude Profile test scores and the interrelationships between first, second, and third year aptitude and achievement results were formally investigated.

*Validity Criteria*

The initial musical achievement test, constructed for the purpose of evaluating the extent to which pupils had learned specific literacy concepts generally taught as part of the first-year instructional program in instrumental music, consisted of four subtests: Melodic Recognition, Rhythmic Recognition, Harmonic Recognition, and Symbolic Understanding. The first subtest, Melodic Recognition, was designed to measure the abil-

[7]

ity to recognize, in various major and minor keys, the musical notation of a phrase heard on a tape recording. Two short musical phrases, rhythmically similar but melodically different, were given notationally, in both the treble and bass clefs, in a test booklet. The students were given recorded directions to indicate on an answer sheet whether the first phrase given, the second phrase given, or neither was actually performed on the tape. The taped phrase was performed twice to afford students an opportunity to read each notational phrase as they listened to the performance. A clarinet, saxophone, bassoon, oboe, trumpet, violin, cello, and a soprano voice were utilized as performance media.

The Rhythmic Recognition test, similar in design to the Melodic Recognition test, differed in that the notational phrases in the treble clef, with various duple, triple, mixed, and unusual meter signatures, were alike melodically but different rhythmically. The Harmonic Recognition test was similar in design to the first two tests. In this test, however, the notational phrases in the treble clef were alike in melody and rhythm, but different in terms of the chord letter names which indicated the simple harmony performed on a ukelele. Only tonic, subdominant, and dominant-seventh chords were utilized.

The Symbolic Understanding test was not a listening test, although the test directions were recorded. On each of ten pages in the test booklet, five multiple-choice questions were asked about a short musical phrase which was written in musical notation at the top of the page. The questions pertained to meanings and definitions associated with key and meter signatures, note names, note values, repeat signs, dynamic signs, tempo markings, and the like.

This musical achievement test was developed during the first year the longitudinal study was in progress. During that year, a preliminary "tryout" was conducted in Muscatine, Iowa. The quality of each item was checked by application of standard item analysis techniques and the test was refined on the basis of the resulting findings.

The specific directions given to the teachers for evaluating the overall musical achievement of their students on a seven-point rating scale, may be found in Appendix A. The five-point rating scale form used by the judges for evaluating the melodic, rhythmic, and expressive aspects of the three tape-recorded performances each year by each student is given in Appendix B. The judges were directed to listen to a sample of the tape-recorded performances before they actually began to compare the achievement of students. As can be discerned from the suggestions given on the rating scale in Appendix B, the judges were given the necessary musical freedom for adequately evaluating the tape-recorded performances of the students.

[8]

The three etudes which the students performed at the end of each of the three years of the study are given in Appendix C. The difficulty levels of the specially composed etudes correspond, in general, to that of the music which was used in group lessons in the schools during each year. However, in an attempt to allow every student to demonstrate whatever ability he had achieved, each etude was designed to progress in difficulty from beginning to end. The technical demands of each etude were made as nearly comparable as possible for all instruments.

## RESULTS OF THE FIRST YEAR OF THE STUDY

*Aptitude Test Results*

As stated, the Musical Aptitude Profile was administered to all 241 students (211 were enrolled in fifth grade and thirty in fourth grade) before they received any formal instruction in school instrumental music. The battery was administered in individual classrooms during October, 1963. The pretraining standard score means and standard deviations for the students in each of the five participating schools and the total group combined are presented in Table 1.

A comparison of the means and standard deviations found for the total experimental group with the means and standard deviations obtained for the general sample of fifth-grade students on whom the standardization was based shows a high degree of similarity. It is not unreasonable to assume, therefore, that the fifth-grade students who participated in this longitudinal predictive validity study are representative of the general population of students for whom the Musical Aptitude Profile is appropriate in actual practice. The one group of fourth-grade students (School 1) that participated in this study scored slightly higher on the average than fourth-grade students in general.

The raw score split-halves (Spearman-Brown corrected) reliability coefficients for the pretraining administration of the Musical Aptitude Profile are presented in Table 2 for each of the five schools and for the total group. The within-schools coefficients for the total group are also given in the last column of this table. The within-schools reliability coefficients were calculated in order to "partial out" the effect of possible overall school and grade differences among the groups of students. However, the pupil groups were so similar that no substantial differences between total and within-group coefficients were observed. In general, the reliability coefficients are of approximately the same magnitude as those which had previously been found for larger and more heterogeneous groups of students.

[9]

## Table 1

Standard Score Means and Standard Deviations for the Pretraining Administration (October, 1963) of the Musical Aptitude Profile for Each of the Five Schools and the Total Group

| | School 1 N=30 | | School 2 N=55 | | School 3 N=44 | | School 4 N=50 | | School 5 N=62 | | Total Group N=241 | |
|---|---|---|---|---|---|---|---|---|---|---|---|---|
| | Mean | SD | Mean | SD | Mean | SD | Mean | SD | Mean | SD | Mean | SD |
| $T_1$: Melody | 44.6 | 9.99 | 50.2 | 9.99 | 43.6 | 7.61 | 48.2 | 9.78 | 47.0 | 8.82 | 46.7 | 9.68 |
| $T_2$: Harmony | 47.5 | 9.98 | 51.9 | 9.69 | 42.3 | 6.87 | 46.9 | 8.35 | 46.3 | 7.85 | 47.0 | 9.37 |
| T: Tonal Imagery | 46.0 | 9.96 | 51.0 | 8.81 | 42.9 | 6.15 | 47.5 | 7.69 | 46.6 | 6.98 | 46.8 | 8.45 |
| $R_1$: Tempo | 47.3 | 7.04 | 48.7 | 8.45 | 42.9 | 6.35 | 45.9 | 8.32 | 49.0 | 8.49 | 46.8 | 8.19 |
| $R_2$: Meter | 45.5 | 7.27 | 46.0 | 9.45 | 41.6 | 4.73 | 44.5 | 7.52 | 47.3 | 8.54 | 45.0 | 8.00 |
| R: Rhythm Imagery | 46.4 | 6.26 | 47.3 | 8.36 | 42.2 | 4.91 | 45.2 | 7.16 | 48.1 | 7.95 | 45.8 | 7.42 |
| $S_1$: Phrasing | 44.9 | 7.61 | 50.6 | 8.00 | 45.0 | 8.16 | 46.2 | 8.72 | 51.3 | 9.74 | 47.6 | 8.92 |
| $S_2$: Balance | 44.1 | 9.75 | 48.3 | 9.85 | 44.0 | 7.29 | 46.5 | 7.86 | 50.1 | 9.99 | 46.6 | 9.30 |
| $S_3$: Style | 45.4 | 7.83 | 47.3 | 8.72 | 41.4 | 7.45 | 44.5 | 7.66 | 49.3 | 8.77 | 45.6 | 8.51 |
| S: Musical Sensitivity | 44.8 | 6.44 | 48.7 | 6.77 | 43.5 | 7.44 | 45.7 | 6.90 | 50.2 | 8.17 | 46.6 | 7.31 |
| C: Composite | 45.7 | 6.50 | 49.0 | 6.88 | 42.9 | 6.08 | 46.1 | 5.69 | 48.3 | 6.45 | 46.4 | 6.40 |

[10]

## Table 2

Reliability Coefficients for the Pretraining Administration (October, 1963) of the Musical Aptitude Profile for Each of the Five Schools and the Total Group

|  |  | School 1 | School 2 | School 3 | School 4 | School 5 | Total Group | Within-Schools |
|---|---|---|---|---|---|---|---|---|
| | $T_1$: Melody | .81 | .84 | .74 | .81 | .81 | .81 | .80 |
| | $T_2$: Harmony | .81 | .84 | .64 | .71 | .78 | .73 | .70 |
| T: | Tonal Imagery | .92 | .90 | .80 | .83 | .86 | .87 | .86 |
| | $R_1$: Tempo | .76 | .78 | .65 | .86 | .80 | .78 | .77 |
| | $R_2$: Meter | .73 | .77 | .60 | .81 | .72 | .73 | .70 |
| R: | Rhythm Imagery | .80 | .85 | .76 | .92 | .82 | .83 | .82 |
| | $S_1$: Phrasing | .73 | .73 | .64 | .70 | .76 | .70 | .70 |
| | $S_2$: Balance | .72 | .72 | .60 | .85 | .72 | .70 | .70 |
| | $S_3$: Style | .76 | .72 | .60 | .84 | .72 | .70 | .70 |
| S: | Musical Sensitivity | .82 | .87 | .78 | .92 | .84 | .86 | .86 |
| C: | Composite | .94 | .93 | .87 | .92 | .91 | .92 | .92 |

## Achievement Test Results

After the students participating in the predictive study had received one academic year of instrumental music instruction, they were given the musical achievement test (May, 1964). The achievement test means and standard deviations for each of the five schools and the total group are presented in Table 3.

It can be observed that the means are about half—in some cases slightly more than half—the possible score. It can be assumed then, that the difficulty level of the tests was not inappropriate. The magnitude of the standard deviations suggests that the variability of each test was sufficient to provide for adequate discrimination among the individual students. The split-halves reliability coefficients (Spearman-Brown corrected) of each test for students in each of the five schools and for the total group are given in Table 4. The within-schools reliability coefficients (given in the last column of Table 4) were also calculated in order to "partial out" the possible effects of overall differences in training procedures associated with particular schools as well as the possible effects of overall age differences among the groups. These reliability coefficients are on the whole of such magnitude as to lend considerable support to those validity coefficients reported in the following pages which involve performance on the achievement battery as the criterion.

The predictive validity coefficients for Musical Aptitude Profile scores obtained in October, 1963, with musical achievement test scores obtained

[11]

### Table 3

Raw Score Means and Standard Deviations for Each of the Five Schools and the Total Group for the Musical Achievement Test Administered (May, 1964) After One Year of Instrumental Music Instruction

| | Items | School 1 | | School 2 | | School 3 | | School 4 | | School 5 | | Total Group | |
|---|---|---|---|---|---|---|---|---|---|---|---|---|---|
| | | Mean | SD | Mean | SD | Mean | SD | Mean | SD | Mean | SD | Mean | SD |
| Melodic Recognition | 28 | 18.4 | 4.61 | 18.0 | 5.70 | 13.3 | 4.27 | 16.6 | 4.91 | 15.7 | 4.93 | 16.4 | 5.10 |
| Rhythmic Recognition | 28 | 16.4 | 5.33 | 15.9 | 4.81 | 12.8 | 3.65 | 15.9 | 4.20 | 14.5 | 4.94 | 15.1 | 4.71 |
| Harmonic Recognition | 28 | 13.8 | 4.46 | 14.1 | 4.23 | 11.8 | 3.36 | 12.8 | 3.81 | 12.6 | 4.43 | 13.0 | 4.10 |
| Symbolic Understanding | 48 | 27.9 | 7.56 | 28.4 | 7.38 | 22.0 | 5.47 | 27.4 | 7.16 | 25.1 | 6.73 | 26.2 | 6.93 |
| Composite | 132 | 76.5 | 16.69 | 76.4 | 18.73 | 59.9 | 12.27 | 72.7 | 16.17 | 67.9 | 16.57 | 70.7 | 16.43 |

## Table 4

### Reliability Coefficients for Each of the Five Schools and the Total Group for the Musical Achievement Test Administered (May, 1964) After One Year of Instrumental Music Instruction

|  | School 1 | School 2 | School 3 | School 4 | School 5 | Total Group | Within-Schools |
|---|---|---|---|---|---|---|---|
| Melodic Recognition | .82 | .87 | .70 | .76 | .84 | .81 | .80 |
| Rhythmic Recognition | .80 | .81 | .70 | .77 | .80 | .79 | .77 |
| Harmonic Recognition | .79 | .73 | .60 | .60 | .72 | .69 | .68 |
| Symbolic Understanding | .80 | .73 | .60 | .72 | .74 | .81 | .80 |
| Composite | .83 | .88 | .79 | .84 | .89 | .91 | .90 |

## Table 5

### First-Year Within-Schools Predictive Validity Coefficients for the Musical Aptitude Profile with Musical Achievement Test Scores as Criteria

|  | Achievement Test | | | | |
|---|---|---|---|---|---|
|  | Melodic Recognition | Rhythmic Recognition | Harmonic Recognition | Symbolic Understanding | Composite |
| Aptitude Test |  |  |  |  |  |
| $T_1$: Melody | .41 | .24 | .30 | .37 | .46 |
| $T_2$: Harmony | .33 | .24 | .38 | .33 | .44 |
| T: Tonal Imagery | .41 | .27 | .38 | .39 | .50 |
| $R_1$: Tempo | .37 | .29 | .28 | .39 | .43 |
| $R_2$: Meter | .45 | .32 | .37 | .40 | .50 |
| R: Rhythm Imagery | .45 | .34 | .36 | .44 | .51 |
| $S_1$: Phrasing | .32 | .27 | .22 | .23 | .31 |
| $S_2$: Balance | .42 | .38 | .27 | .37 | .47 |
| $S_3$: Style | .35 | .35 | .29 | .38 | .47 |
| S: Musical Sensitivity | .45 | .41 | .32 | .40 | .51 |
| C: Composite | .53 | .41 | .42 | .49 | .61 |

in May, 1964, used as criteria, may be found for each school and for the total group in Appendix D. The within-schools validity coefficients, again calculated to "partial out" the possible effects of overall differences in training procedures and age differences among groups, are reported in Table 5.

While there is considerable variation among the predictive validity coefficients for the five different schools, the coefficients obtained for each school tend to approximate those reported for the total group. Also, the within-group coefficients are quite similar in magnitude to those obtained

[13]

for the total group. On the whole, the validity of the composite scores on the Musical Aptitude Profile for predicting achievement in recognition of musical notation and the understanding of musical signs and symbols is quite high, especially in view of the fact that they were obtained after only one year of formal instruction in instrumental music.

Generally, the aptitude subtests appeared to have similar power for predicting achievement. The one exception was Test $S_1$ (Musical Sensitivity—Phrasing) which consistently exhibited the least predictive validity. As would be expected, the Tonal, Rhythm, and Sensitivity totals had higher predictive validity coefficients than the subtests, and the composite score displayed the highest predictive validity of all.

*Performance and Teacher Rating Results*

Students were rated on the melodic, rhythmic, and expressive aspects of their tape-recorded performances on each of three etudes. A five-point rating scale was used for each aspect. Because fifteen points could be awarded by each judge for each etude performed and because each student performed each of the three etudes twice (i.e., one set of three performances in one week and a second set the following week), a student could earn a possible grand total of 180 points. Means and standard deviations of the combined ratings of both judges for both performances of each etude as well as for all three etudes are presented in Table 6. Also given in this table are the means and standard deviations of each teacher's seven-point rating of the musical achievement and progress of his individual students. There is an amazing consistency in the rank order of the school means of achievement test scores and teacher ratings. School 1, which was in second position on the basis of the teacher rating, was in first position on the basis of the achievement test and School 2, which was in second position on the achievement test, was in first position on the teacher rating scale; the positions of the other three schools were the same on both counts. However, the rank order consistency of the schools when all three criteria are considered is, except for School 3, somewhat different. School 1 was ranked first by the judges and the test but second by the teacher; School 2, which was ranked first by the teacher and second by the test, was ranked fourth by the judges; School 4 was ranked third by the test and the teacher but second by the judges; and School 5 was ranked fourth by the test and the teacher but third by the judges. In connection with this rank order consistency analysis, it should be understood that these inter-school criteria comparisons necessarily lack precision because students in all five schools were evaluated by the same judges and with the same test, but each teacher rated only his own students. Although a with-

[14]

## Table 6

Means and Standard Deviations for Students' Performances of All
Tape-Recorded Etudes and Teacher Ratings for the First Year

|  | School 1 Mean | SD | School 2 Mean | SD | School 3 Mean | SD | School 4 Mean | SD | School 5 Mean | SD | Total Group Mean | SD |
|---|---|---|---|---|---|---|---|---|---|---|---|---|
| Etude 1 (With Help) | 37.0 | 7.76 | 28.1 | 11.29 | 21.1 | 11.73 | 32.3 | 10.84 | 27.2 | 13.45 | 29.1 | 11.56 |
| Etude 2 (Without Help) | 36.8 | 9.96 | 28.0 | 11.16 | 20.9 | 12.12 | 33.6 | 11.67 | 31.7 | 14.04 | 30.2 | 12.12 |
| Etude 3 (Sight Reading) | 33.9 | 8.63 | 25.7 | 10.42 | 16.8 | 8.87 | 28.7 | 11.28 | 26.8 | 13.72 | 26.4 | 11.10 |
| All Etudes | 107.7 | 24.91 | 81.8 | 32.46 | 58.8 | 31.97 | 94.6 | 32.45 | 85.7 | 39.84 | 85.7 | 41.22 |
| Teacher Ratings | 4.4 | 1.72 | 4.9 | 1.71 | 3.1 | 1.87 | 4.3 | 1.87 | 3.3 | 1.83 | 4.0 | 1.83 |

## Table 7

### Correlations Between Judges' Evaluation of Students' Tape-Recorded Instrumental Music Performances for the First Year

| | School 1 | School 2 | School 3 | School 4 | School 5 | Total Group | Within-Schools |
|---|---|---|---|---|---|---|---|
| *First Week* | | | | | | | |
| Etude 1 (With Help) | .70 | .83 | .85 | .65 | .79 | .73 | .73 |
| Etude 2 (Without Help) | .90 | .77 | .88 | .72 | .76 | .77 | .78 |
| Etude 3 (Sight Reading) | .89 | .72 | .76 | .67 | .77 | .76 | .75 |
| All Etudes | .89 | .81 | .87 | .72 | .84 | .80 | .80 |
| *Second Week* | | | | | | | |
| Etude 1 (With Help) | .68 | .85 | .88 | .65 | .82 | .78 | .78 |
| Etude 2 (Without Help) | .73 | .85 | .88 | .68 | .81 | .78 | .78 |
| Etude 3 (Sight Reading) | .61 | .85 | .87 | .72 | .79 | .78 | .77 |
| All Etudes | .72 | .88 | .94 | .72 | .86 | .83 | .83 |
| *First and Second Week* | | | | | | | |
| All Etudes | .89 | .87 | .93 | .81 | .89 | .85 | .85 |

in-schools analysis is applicable for correlation purposes, it does not provide for an analysis of the comparability of means.

The reliabilities of the two judges' evaluations of the tape-recorded student performances are presented in Table 7. The test-retest reliabilities of the students' tape-recorded performances as estimated from their renditions of the same music during two adjacent weeks are given in Table 8. The relationships between judges' ratings are very high and the relationships between the students' two tape-recorded performances are even higher. Undoubtedly, the high reliability of these ratings contributed to the substantial predictive validity coefficients presented in the following tables. The design of the study did not provide for an assessment of the reliability of the teacher ratings. It is possible that the lower validity coefficients which were found when teachers' ratings were used as the criterion may in part, at least, be due to relatively low reliability of these ratings.

### Predictive Validity Results

The validity coefficients for the Musical Aptitude Profile as a predictor

[16]

## Table 8

### Correlations Between Students' Tape-Recorded Instrumental Music Performances on Two Adjacent Weeks for the First Year

|  | School 1 | School 2 | School 3 | School 4 | School 5 | Total Group | Within-Schools |
|---|---|---|---|---|---|---|---|
| *Judge One* |  |  |  |  |  |  |  |
| Etude 1 (With Help) | .90 | .69 | .90 | .85 | .76 | .82 | .81 |
| Etude 2 (Without Help) | .91 | .72 | .93 | .89 | .81 | .86 | .86 |
| Etude 3 (Sight Reading) | .81 | .68 | .82 | .81 | .72 | .76 | .75 |
| All Etudes | .92 | .74 | .95 | .88 | .88 | .89 | .89 |
| *Judge Two* |  |  |  |  |  |  |  |
| Etude 1 (With Help) | .86 | .64 | .89 | .73 | .86 | .83 | .81 |
| Etude 2 (Without Help) | .88 | .70 | .83 | .74 | .80 | .83 | .79 |
| Etude 3 (Sight Reading) | .87 | .72 | .83 | .71 | .84 | .82 | .79 |
| All Etudes | .81 | .72 | .91 | .77 | .89 | .87 | .85 |

of success in instrumental music, as measured by judges' ratings of tape-recorded student performances, may be found for each of the five schools and for the total group in Appendix E. The within-schools predictive validity coefficients are given in Table 9. In addition, the validity coefficients for the Musical Aptitude Profile as a predictor of music teachers' ratings of student achievement and progress in instrumental music are also given in Table 9 and corresponding tables in Appendix E. For convenience of comparison, the correlation coefficients between Musical Aptitude Profile test scores and the composite musical achievement test scores which were previously presented are repeated in Table 9 and corresponding tables in Appendix E. Finally, scores for the three tape-recorded performances, teacher ratings, and the musical achievement composite were combined for each student into an unweighted Grand Composite. The correlation coefficients, which represent the relationship between this Grand Composite score and Musical Aptitude Profile scores, are also shown for individual schools and the total group in Appendix E and for within-schools in Table 9.

The one year predictive validity coefficients reported in Table 9 are high even in comparison with concurrent validity coefficients which are generally reported for other aptitude tests. Aptitude test scores predicted achievement test scores somewhat better than they predicted instrumental

# Table 9

First-Year Within-Schools Validity Coefficients for the Musical Aptitude Profile as a Predictor of Judges' Evaluations of Instrumental Music Tape-Recorded Performances, Teacher Ratings, and Musical Achievement Composite Test Scores

| | Melody $T_1$ | Harmony $T_2$ | Tonal Imagery $T$ | Tempo $R_1$ | Meter $R_2$ | Rhythm Imagery $R$ | Phrasing $S_1$ | Balance $S_2$ | Style $S_3$ | Musical Sensitivity $S$ | Composite $C$ |
|---|---|---|---|---|---|---|---|---|---|---|---|
| **Judges' Ratings** | | | | | | | | | | | |
| Etude 1 (With Help) | .38 | .31 | .39 | .35 | .40 | .42 | .30 | .37 | .38 | .43 | .49 |
| Etude 2 (Without Help) | .38 | .32 | .40 | .39 | .43 | .45 | .28 | .43 | .40 | .46 | .52 |
| Etude 3 (Sight Reading) | .39 | .33 | .40 | .34 | .40 | .41 | .30 | .43 | .40 | .47 | .51 |
| All Etudes | .39 | .33 | .41 | .37 | .42 | .44 | .30 | .42 | .41 | .47 | .53 |
| Teacher Ratings | .26 | .24 | .28 | .26 | .30 | .31 | .22 | .32 | .26 | .33 | .37 |
| Achievement Test | .46 | .44 | .50 | .43 | .50 | .51 | .31 | .47 | .47 | .51 | .61 |
| Grand Composite | .45 | .39 | .47 | .42 | .48 | .50 | .33 | .47 | .46 | .52 | .60 |

performances, in spite of the fact that all criteria (except possibly the teachers' ratings) were about equally reliable. The weakest relationships were found between teacher ratings and aptitude scores. It has been suggested that this may be due in part to the possible lack of reliability of these ratings. However, it may also be attributable to possible weakness in their validity; that is, to the extramusical factors which teachers might have considered in their rating of students' achievement or to the teacher's relative lack of ability to discriminate among students with similar but not "equal" talent. The within-schools intercorrelations between the various validity criteria were .75 for all etudes and teacher ratings, .66 for all etudes and the achievement test composite, and .49 for the achievement test composite and teacher ratings.

To provide a simpler and perhaps sharper picture of the power of the Musical Aptitude Profile as a predictor of success in musical endeavors, the students scoring among the upper and lower tenth on the aptitude test were identified. The composite mean scores for the various validity criteria for these two extreme groups of students, as well as for all students who participated in the study, are presented in Table 10. It is clear that the Musical Aptitude Profile discriminates sharply among students in terms

## Table 10

### First-Year Composite Mean Scores for the 10 Per Cent Highest and 10 Per Cent Lowest Scoring Students and for the Total Group

|  | Musical Aptitude Profile | All Etudes | Teacher Ratings | Achievement Test | Grand Composite |
|---|---|---|---|---|---|
| Upper 10% | 57.3 | 122.0 | 5.3 | 92.0 | 219.3 |
| Total Group | 46.4 | 85.8 | 4.0 | 70.2 | 160.0 |
| Lower 10% | 35.2 | 56.2 | 3.0 | 53.5 | 112.7 |

of predicting their success after one year of instruction on a musical instrument.

### RESULTS OF THE SECOND YEAR OF THE STUDY

The procedures for evaluating students' progress at the end of the second year of formal instruction were of exactly the same type as those employed the first year. Of course, the students were given more advanced etudes to perform. In addition, the second-year musical achievement test was designed to include content that constituted understandings to which second-year instrumental music students are exposed. Additional items, more musically heterogeneous in character, were developed. Using try-out data and standard test development and item selection procedures, the three recognition tests were each increased from twenty-eight to forty-four items and the Symbolic Understanding test from forty-eight to fifty items. Thus, the musical achievement test used for the second year of the study contained a total of 182 items, an increase of fifty items over the first-year test.

In spite of the fact that one of the criteria considered in making the original choice of participating schools was neighborhood stability, some students moved away from their respective school districts, with the result that the number of students who participated in the second year of the study was reduced from 241 to 213—a total loss of twenty-eight students for the five schools combined.

*Achievement Test Results*

The means and standard deviations for the musical achievement test, administered in May, 1965, are presented for the five schools and the total group in Table 11. The means are not inconsistent with generally accepted test difficulty standards and the standard deviations are sufficiently large to suggest that the tests did indeed effectually differentiate among the

[19]

## Table 11

Raw Score Means and Standard Deviations for Each of the Five Schools and the Total Group on the Musical Achievement Test Administered (May, 1965) After Two Years of Instrumental Music Instruction

| | Items | School 1 N=30 | | School 2 N=48 | | School 3 N=41 | | School 4 N=41 | | School 5 N=53 | | Total Group N=213 | |
|---|---|---|---|---|---|---|---|---|---|---|---|---|---|
| | | Mean | SD | Mean | SD | Mean | SD | Mean | SD | Mean | SD | Mean | SD |
| Melodic Recognition | 44 | 31.6 | 6.62 | 29.4 | 7.55 | 22.9 | 6.54 | 27.4 | 6.81 | 25.6 | 6.80 | 27.4 | 7.45 |
| Rhythmic Recognition | 44 | 27.4 | 6.99 | 25.7 | 7.30 | 19.7 | 6.07 | 25.6 | 7.21 | 23.4 | 6.04 | 24.4 | 7.16 |
| Harmonic Recognition | 44 | 26.7 | 5.99 | 25.2 | 6.04 | 18.9 | 4.93 | 23.7 | 6.96 | 20.6 | 6.32 | 23.0 | 6.70 |
| Symbolic Understanding | 50 | 32.8 | 7.16 | 30.1 | 7.99 | 23.6 | 5.96 | 30.9 | 7.51 | 27.6 | 7.00 | 29.0 | 7.76 |
| Composite | 182 | 118.5 | 22.96 | 110.4 | 24.98 | 85.1 | 19.03 | 107.6 | 24.76 | 97.2 | 20.53 | 103.8 | 24.98 |

[20]

## Table 12

Reliability Coefficients for Each of the Five Schools and the Total Group
for the Musical Achievement Test Administered (May, 1965) After Two
Years of Instrumental Music Instruction

|  | School 1 | School 2 | School 3 | School 4 | School 5 | Total Group | Within-Schools |
|---|---|---|---|---|---|---|---|
| Melodic Recognition | .86 | .87 | .82 | .85 | .85 | .87 | .85 |
| Rhythmic Recognition | .81 | .76 | .78 | .87 | .82 | .83 | .81 |
| Harmonic Recognition | .85 | .70 | .77 | .80 | .77 | .81 | .79 |
| Symbolic Understanding | .75 | .87 | .77 | .93 | .73 | .84 | .81 |
| Composite | .94 | .95 | .92 | .96 | .93 | .95 | .94 |

## Table 13

Second-Year Within-Schools Predictive Validity Coefficients for the Musical
Aptitude Profile with Musical Achievement Test Scores as Criteria

|  | Achievement Test | | | | |
|---|---|---|---|---|---|
|  | Melodic Recognition | Rhythmic Recognition | Harmonic Recognition | Symbolic Understanding | Composite |
| *Aptitude Test* | | | | | |
| $T_1$: Melody | .45 | .33 | .24 | .29 | .40 |
| $T_2$: Harmony | .40 | .33 | .32 | .26 | .40 |
| T: Tonal Imagery | .45 | .38 | .31 | .32 | .44 |
| $R_1$: Tempo | .39 | .31 | .31 | .31 | .41 |
| $R_2$: Meter | .47 | .36 | .38 | .38 | .49 |
| R: Rhythm Imagery | .47 | .38 | .38 | .37 | .49 |
| $S_1$: Phrasing | .29 | .22 | .26 | .27 | .31 |
| $S_2$: Balance | .46 | .41 | .41 | .44 | .52 |
| $S_3$: Style | .44 | .36 | .41 | .41 | .49 |
| S: Musical Sensitivity | .48 | .41 | .45 | .46 | .54 |
| C: Composite | .57 | .47 | .46 | .46 | .61 |

students. The reliability coefficients given in Table 12 are considerably
higher than those reported for the test used at the end of the first year of
the study.

The predictive validity coefficients for October, 1963, Musical Aptitude
Profile scores, with May, 1965, musical achievement test scores used as
criteria, may be found for each school and for the total group in Appendix
D. The within-schools validity coefficients are reported in Table 13. A
comparison of these predictive validity coefficients with those reported

when first-year achievement test scores were used as criteria (see Table 5) shows that, in general, the degree of prediction over a two-year period was similar to the degree of prediction over a one-year period. Usually a shrinkage in the magnitude of the predictive validity coefficients would be expected to occur with an increase in the interval of time between testings. In this study two things may have counteracted such shrinkage; the second-year achievement test is definitely more reliable, and the additional year of musical training should have increased individual differences in accomplishment in a manner that is to some degree consistent with differences in aptitude. It is interesting to note that the within-schools coefficients for composite aptitude and achievement test scores were exactly the same for both years and that, in general, relationships among aptitude and achievement subtests were similar in magnitude.

## Performance and Teacher Rating Results

Performance means and standard deviations for all second-year etudes for both performances combined are presented in Table 14. Means and standard deviations of teacher ratings are also given in Table 14.

Although there was some change in the rank order of the schools on the basis of the judges' evaluations of student performance, School 3 continued to remain conspicuously low. Overall, the performance ratings were somewhat higher than at the end of the first year, indicating that in the judges' opinion the ability of the students to perform was improving. The means and standard deviations of the teacher ratings were very similar to those of the first year.

The reliability coefficients, indicative of the degree to which the two judges agreed in their evaluations of second-year tape-recorded performances, are presented in Table 15. The test-retest reliabilities of the students' second-year tape-recorded performances, as estimated from their renditions of the same music during two adjacent weeks, are given in Table 16. As for the first year, the reliability of teacher ratings could not be directly estimated.

## Predictive Validity Results

The second-year predictive validity coefficients for the Musical Aptitude Profile, with judges' evaluations of students' tape-recorded performances as the criterion, may be found for each of the five schools and for the total group in Appendix E. The within-schools predictive validity coefficients are given in Table 17. In addition, the validity coefficients, with music teacher ratings of student achievement and progress in instrumental music as the criterion, are also given in Table 17 and corresponding tables in Ap-

# Table 14

## Means and Standard Deviations for Students' Performances of All Tape-Recorded Etudes and Teacher Ratings for the Second Year

| | School 1 | | School 2 | | School 3 | | School 4 | | School 5 | | Total Group | |
|---|---|---|---|---|---|---|---|---|---|---|---|---|
| | Mean | SD | Mean | SD | Mean | SD | Mean | SD | Mean | SD | Mean | SD |
| Etude 1 (With Help) | 36.0 | 9.40 | 37.9 | 11.05 | 19.2 | 11.94 | 36.5 | 12.84 | 28.0 | 15.38 | 31.5 | 14.38 |
| Etude 2 (Without Help) | 30.9 | 9.45 | 35.5 | 10.34 | 18.6 | 11.36 | 33.0 | 11.12 | 27.4 | 15.06 | 29.1 | 13.31 |
| Etude 3 (Sight Reading) | 31.6 | 10.31 | 36.6 | 11.14 | 18.4 | 11.16 | 34.4 | 12.40 | 27.1 | 15.21 | 29.6 | 14.01 |
| All Etudes | 98.5 | 28.51 | 110.0 | 32.13 | 56.2 | 34.11 | 103.9 | 35.30 | 82.5 | 45.28 | 90.2 | 41.19 |
| Teacher Ratings | 3.9 | 1.82 | 4.8 | 1.71 | 1.7 | 1.41 | 3.8 | 1.98 | 2.7 | 1.97 | 3.4 | 2.10 |

[23]

## Table 15

### Correlations Between Judges' Evaluations of Students' Tape-Recorded Instrumental Music Performances for the Second Year

|  | School 1 | School 2 | School 3 | School 4 | School 5 | Total Group | Within-Schools |
|---|---|---|---|---|---|---|---|
| *First Week* |  |  |  |  |  |  |  |
| Etude 1 (With Help) | .88 | .82 | .87 | .81 | .91 | .87 | .85 |
| Etude 2 (Without Help) | .89 | .80 | .84 | .90 | .91 | .87 | .85 |
| Etude 3 (Sight Reading) | .95 | .88 | .89 | .94 | .94 | .92 | .91 |
| All Etudes | .91 | .86 | .85 | .89 | .93 | .90 | .88 |
| *Second Week* |  |  |  |  |  |  |  |
| Etude 1 (With Help) | .87 | .92 | .88 | .84 | .90 | .88 | .87 |
| Etude 2 (Without Help) | .87 | .90 | .78 | .88 | .94 | .88 | .86 |
| Etude 3 (Sight Reading) | .89 | .93 | .86 | .93 | .96 | .92 | .90 |
| All Etudes | .95 | .93 | .87 | .95 | .96 | .93 | .92 |
| *First and Second Weeks* |  |  |  |  |  |  |  |
| All Etudes | .94 | .94 | .89 | .94 | .95 | .96 | .95 |

## Table 16

### Correlations Between Students' Tape-Recorded Instrumental Music Performances on Two Adjacent Weeks for the Second Year

|  | School 1 | School 2 | School 3 | School 4 | School 5 | Total Group | Within-Schools |
|---|---|---|---|---|---|---|---|
| *Judge One* |  |  |  |  |  |  |  |
| Etude 1 (With Help) | .93 | .95 | .95 | .92 | .95 | .95 | .94 |
| Etude 2 (Without Help) | .94 | .92 | .94 | .91 | .95 | .94 | .93 |
| Etude 3 (Sight Reading) | .94 | .94 | .92 | .93 | .95 | .95 | .94 |
| All Etudes | .96 | .95 | .95 | .96 | .96 | .96 | .95 |
| *Judge Two* |  |  |  |  |  |  |  |
| Etude 1 (With Help) | .89 | .89 | .96 | .91 | .95 | .94 | .93 |
| Etude 2 (Without Help) | .92 | .80 | .95 | .90 | .96 | .93 | .92 |
| Etude 3 (Sight Reading) | .82 | .85 | .95 | .91 | .94 | .93 | .91 |
| All Etudes | .91 | .88 | .96 | .94 | .96 | .95 | .94 |

[24]

Table 17

Second-Year Within-Schools Validity Coefficients for the Musical Aptitude
Profile as a Predictor of Judges' Evaluations of Instrumental Music Tape-
Recorded Performances, Teacher Ratings, and Musical Achievement
Composite Test Scores

| | Melody | Harmony | Tonal Imagery | Tempo | Meter | Rhythm Imagery | Phrasing | Balance | Style | Musical Sensitivity | Composite |
|---|---|---|---|---|---|---|---|---|---|---|---|
| | $T_1$ | $T_2$ | T | $R_1$ | $R_2$ | R | $S_1$ | $S_2$ | $S_3$ | S | C |
| Judges' Ratings | | | | | | | | | | | |
| Etude 1 (With Help) | .46 | .43 | .50 | .43 | .57 | .54 | .42 | .51 | .52 | .61 | .67 |
| Etude 2 (Without Help) | .45 | .43 | .51 | .47 | .58 | .57 | .44 | .53 | .54 | .63 | .69 |
| Etude 3 (Sight Reading) | .46 | .44 | .52 | .47 | .57 | .56 | .46 | .53 | .53 | .63 | .69 |
| All Etudes | .46 | .44 | .52 | .46 | .58 | .57 | .45 | .53 | .54 | .63 | .69 |
| Teacher Ratings | .20 | .17 | .22 | .16 | .26 | .23 | .23 | .32 | .31 | .36 | .39 |
| Achievement Test | .40 | .40 | .44 | .41 | .49 | .49 | .31 | .52 | .49 | .54 | .61 |
| Grand Composite | .47 | .45 | .52 | .47 | .58 | .57 | .42 | .56 | .66 | .64 | .70 |

pendix E. Again, for convenience in comparison, the correlation coefficients
between Musical Aptitude Profile test scores and the second-year composite musical achievement test scores previously presented are repeated
in Table 17 and corresponding tables in Appendix E. Finally, scores for
the three tape-recorded performances, teacher ratings, and the musical
achievement composite were again combined for each student into an unweighted Grand Composite. The correlation coefficients representing the
relationship between the Grand Composite and Musical Aptitude Profile
scores are also shown for individual schools and the total group in Appendix E and for within-schools in Table 17.

A comparison of Table 17 with similar first-year data (see Table 9)
demonstrates that scores on the Musical Aptitude Profile predict judges'
ratings of instrumental performances after two years of instruction with
considerably more percision than they predict the ratings made after a
one-year period of instruction. On the basis of this criterion, the students
were clearly—as indeed they should—becoming more and more heterogeneous with respect to performance after this longer period of instruction. As
has been indicated previously, the usual experience in predictive validity
studies is that the greater the time period between obtaining predictor and

criterion scores, the more attenuated the coefficients become. In this study the within-schools coefficients increased for all tape-recorded performances and, of course, for the unweighted Grand Composite of which these recorded performances are a part; but for the achievement test and teacher ratings the coefficients remained much the same as they were at the end of the first year. Possible subconscious evaluation of extramusical factors by teachers, together with a possible lack of reliability, may have combined to cause the validity coefficients for teachers' ratings to be so much lower than the others. Furthermore, it should be remembered that the second-year findings regarding the achievement test are not directly comparable to those of the first because the reliability of the second-year achievement test was higher than that for the first-year test. However, it appears possible that some of the new items introduced may have been too difficult for even the better students, while some of the items retained, which were of appropriate difficulty for beginning students, became too easy for even the less able students after two years of training. The net result of this possibility would be similar to that of a test ceiling effect, which in turn would introduce a certain amount of curvilinearity in the relationship between the aptitude and achievement test scores. Scatter diagrams were indeed consistent with this possibility. Had curvilinear (parabolic) validity coefficients been calculated, their values would undoubtedly have been somewhat larger than those of the linear coefficients reported in Table 17.

The overall predictive validity coefficient of .70 indicates that approximately 50 per cent of the variance associated with success in studying a musical instrument after two years of instruction can be predicted from pretraining Musical Aptitude Profile scores. The corresponding variance after one year of study was 35 per cent.

The initial composite aptitude scores (obtained *before* training) predicted the second-year unweighted Grand Composite criterion score as accurately ($r = .70$) as did first-year teacher ratings ($r = .71$) which, of course, were obtained *after* the teachers had given the students one year of instruction. Composite aptitude scores obtained after one year of training were found to be only negligibly better predictors of success ($r = .72$) than the pretraining composite aptitude scores when the unweighted Grand Composite was used as the criterion.

The within-schools intercorrelations between the various second-year validity criteria were .73 for all etudes and teacher ratings; .71 for all etudes and the achievement test composite; and .59 for the achievement test composite and teacher ratings.

Again, after two years of instruction, the 10 per cent highest and the 10 per cent lowest scoring students on the initial administration of the Musical Aptitude Profile were identified and their second-year criterion scores

## Table 18

### Second-Year Composite Mean Scores for the 10 Per Cent Highest and 10 Per Cent Lowest Scoring Students and for the Total Group

| | Musical Aptitude Profile | All Etudes | Teacher Ratings | Achievement Test | Grand Composite |
|---|---|---|---|---|---|
| Upper 10% | 57.9 | 128.6 | 5.0 | 143.0 | 276.6 |
| Total Group | 46.3 | 102.3 | 3.4 | 90.0 | 195.7 |
| Lower 10% | 34.6 | 76.4 | 2.2 | 50.1 | 128.7 |

obtained. Composite mean scores for the various criteria for these two groups of students as well as for the total group are presented in Table 18. It is patently clear that these extremely different aptitude groups are also extremely different in terms of the various validity criteria. Indeed, in contrast to first-year results, no overlap whatever was found for these groups on the Grand Composite criterion—the highest Grand Composite score in the low group was 192 and the lowest Grand Composite score in the high group 206.

## RESULTS OF THE THIRD YEAR OF THE STUDY

The procedures for evaluating the musical achievement of the 193 students who did not move from their respective school districts and, hence, were able to remain in the study through the third year were of exactly the same type as those used for the first- and second-year evaluations. Again, as at the end of the second year, still more advanced etudes and, through standard test development procedures, a more advanced musical achievement test were developed.

Because it was impossible to achieve unanimity among the various teachers regarding correct answers for certain items to be included in the Symbolic Understanding Test, the test was dropped from the musical achievement test battery. Further, teacher consensus suggested that the design of the Harmonic Recognition Test should be changed. Consequently, instead of utilizing chord symbols for implied harmonies, each item consisted of two phrases with two lines of music, contrapuntal in nature, written in the treble clef above and the bass clef below. As in the melody and rhythm tests, the students were asked to indicate which of the two given phrases was the one performed on the tape recording. The treble clef portions of both lines of each phrase were identical, but the bass clef portions were different. The recorded phrases of the exercises were performed on viola

[27]

and cello. Finally, more comprehensive content was included in the Melodic Recognition Test and the Rhythmic Recognition Test. As with the harmony test, the viola and cello were used in performing the recorded phrases of the items of these subtests. Each of the three subtests was made forty-six items long so that the final musical achievement test battery involved a total of 138 items.

It should be noted that during the third year of the study all participating students (except for the one class that began the study in fourth grade) were enrolled in junior high school. As a result, some students were introduced to new instrumental music instructors. Because instrumental music was compulsory for all students participating in the study and because some of these students did not elect to participate in junior high school music organizations, special arrangements were made to enable these students to meet in separate groups for instruction commensurate with their demonstrated achievement. Students who elected to participate in a junior high school instrumental organization were assigned according to their level of achievement. As during the first two years of the study, students were allowed to take private lessons and they were typically encouraged by their teachers to participate in ensembles and other co-curricular musical activities.

### Achievement Test Results

The means and standard deviations for the subtests of the musical achievement test battery, administered in May, 1966, are presented for the five schools and the total group in Table 19. Means and standard deviations for two composite achievement scores are also given in this table. One of these was formed from a combination of the scores on the Melodic Recognition and Rhythm Recognition subtests and the other involved a combination of these two subtests with the third—Harmonic Recognition.

Examination of the means given in Table 19 shows that the students found the final achievement test to be relatively easy. However, the standard deviations are large in relation to the means and the split-halves reliabilities reported in Table 20 are clearly higher than those found for the two prior tests.

The predictive validity coefficients for Musical Aptitude Profile scores obtained in October, 1963, with musical achievement test scores obtained in May, 1966, used as criteria, may be found for each school and for the total group in Appendix D. The within-schools validity coefficients are reported in Table 21. A comparison of these coefficients with corresponding first-year (see Table 5) and second-year (see Table 13) predictive validity coefficients show that the degree of prediction over a three-year period is substantially higher than over a period of either one or two years. Indeed,

## Table 19

Raw Score Means and Standard Deviations for Each of the Five Schools and the Total Group on the Musical Achievement Test Administered (May, 1966) After Three Years of Instrumental Music Instruction

| | Items | School 1 N=28 | | School 2 N=44 | | School 3 N=37 | | School 4 N=32 | | School 5 N=52 | | Total Group N=193 | |
|---|---|---|---|---|---|---|---|---|---|---|---|---|---|
| | | Mean | SD | Mean | SD | Mean | SD | Mean | SD | Mean | SD | Mean | SD |
| Melodic Recognition | 46 | 35.0 | 5.99 | 34.2 | 6.65 | 25.8 | 7.13 | 31.2 | 6.97 | 28.3 | 8.10 | 30.9 | 7.92 |
| Rhythmic Recognition | 46 | 33.0 | 8.07 | 32.7 | 7.94 | 25.2 | 8.31 | 30.0 | 6.81 | 27.5 | 9.18 | 29.7 | 8.75 |
| Melodic and Rhythmic Recognition | 92 | 68.0 | 13.01 | 66.9 | 13.32 | 51.0 | 14.56 | 61.2 | 12.67 | 55.8 | 16.35 | 60.6 | 15.65 |
| Harmonic Recognition | 46 | 32.5 | 8.36 | 34.1 | 7.74 | 23.2 | 8.71 | 29.9 | 8.57 | 25.4 | 8.80 | 29.0 | 9.44 |
| Composite | 138 | 100.5 | 20.41 | 101.0 | 20.05 | 74.2 | 20.91 | 91.1 | 19.61 | 81.2 | 23.80 | 89.6 | 23.77 |

[29]

## Table 20

### Reliability Coefficients for Each of the Five Schools and the Total Group for the Musical Achievement Test Administered (May, 1966) After Three Years of Instrumental Music Instruction

|  | School 1 | School 2 | School 3 | School 4 | School 5 | Total Group | Within-Schools |
|---|---|---|---|---|---|---|---|
| Melodic Recognition | .92 | .88 | .83 | .84 | .94 | .91 | .89 |
| Rhythmic Recognition | .87 | .86 | .86 | .86 | .91 | .90 | .89 |
| Melodic and Rhythmic Recognition | .93 | .94 | .91 | .94 | .95 | .95 | .94 |
| Harmonic Recognition | .95 | .91 | .90 | .91 | .92 | .94 | .91 |
| Composite | .97 | .97 | .95 | .96 | .95 | .97 | .96 |

## Table 21

### Third-Year Within-Schools Predictive Validity Coefficients for the Musical Aptitude Profile with Musical Achievement Test Scores as Criteria

|  | Melodic Recognition | Rhythmic Recognition | Melodic and Rhythmic Recognition | Harmonic Recognition | Composite |
|---|---|---|---|---|---|
| *Aptitude Test* |  |  |  |  |  |
| $T_1$: Melody | .37 | .40 | .41 | .42 | .44 |
| $T_2$: Harmony | .45 | .45 | .49 | .45 | .50 |
| T: Tonal Imagery | .47 | .50 | .53 | .49 | .54 |
| $R_1$: Tempo | .48 | .40 | .47 | .49 | .51 |
| $R_2$: Meter | .52 | .44 | .52 | .51 | .55 |
| R: Rhythm Imagery | .55 | .47 | .55 | .55 | .58 |
| $S_1$: Phrasing | .46 | .39 | .45 | .43 | .47 |
| $S_2$: Balance | .48 | .40 | .47 | .48 | .50 |
| $S_3$: Style | .42 | .46 | .48 | .45 | .50 |
| S: Musical Sensitivity | .56 | .52 | .58 | .54 | .60 |
| C: Composite | .66 | .61 | .69 | .65 | .71 |

the initial aptitude scores predicted final-year achievement test scores better than they did either the first-year or the second-year Grand Composite criterion.

Although the higher reliabilities of the achievement subtests would account for some of the increase in these higher coefficients, a more likely explanation is that a rather long period of training on a musical instrument is necessary to develop potential or aptitude for achievement to a point at which individual differences become more easily measurable. In this connection, it is of interest that for an independent sample of junior high school students, the concurrent validity coefficient for composite scores on the aptitude test with the final version achievement test composite scores as a criterion was only .53. That is, the within-schools three-year predictive validity coefficient (.71) indicates that pretraining aptitude test composite scores account for about twice as much of the variance of achievement test scores than do aptitude test scores obtained concurrently with achievement test scores.

Apart from the overall difference in magnitude, the pattern of intercorrelation coefficients between the various aptitude test scores and the third-year achievement test scores was, in general, similar to those found for the first and second years. The one obvious exception was the improvement of the predictive power of subtest $S_1$ (Musical Sensitivity—Phrasing) in the third year.

*Performance and Teacher Rating Results*

Performance means and standard deviations for all third-year etudes for both weeks combined are given in Table 22. Means and standard deviations of teacher ratings are reported in the last line of this table. The rank order of the school means is precisely the same for all three criteria, namely, achievement test composite, judges' ratings over all etudes, and teacher ratings of achievement. Again, School 3 was conspicuously low on all measures.

The reliability of the two judges' evaluations of tape-recorded performances of the third-year etudes are presented in Table 23. The test retest reliabilities of the students' third-year tape-recorded performances, as estimated from their renditions of the same music during two adjacent weeks, are given in Table 24. Similiar to the previous two years, the reliability of teacher ratings could again not be directly estimated for final-year data.

The high reliability coefficients found at the end of the second year of the study for both repeated student performances and inter-judge agreement in evaluating these performances were at least equalled for the third year of the study. This is an expected result since the same team of judges that made the second-year evaluations also rated the third-year performances. The contribution of experience to inter-judge reliability is shown by the lower coefficients for the first etudes rated; namely, those performed during the first week at the end of the second year. The coefficients for the second week of the second year and both weeks of the third tended to be slightly higher. Of course, the increasing heterogeneity of the group in

## Table 22

Means and Standard Deviations for Students' Performances of All Tape-Recorded Etudes and Teacher Ratings for the Third Year

|  | School 1 | | School 2 | | School 3 | | School 4 | | School 5 | | Total Group | |
|---|---|---|---|---|---|---|---|---|---|---|---|---|
|  | Mean | SD | Mean | SD | Mean | SD | Mean | SD | Mean | SD | Mean | SD |
| Etude 1 (With Help) | 37.8 | 9.86 | 40.1 | 10.15 | 24.7 | 12.25 | 35.6 | 13.73 | 33.5 | 15.30 | 34.3 | 13.71 |
| Etude 2 (Without Help) | 37.1 | 10.06 | 39.4 | 9.99 | 23.2 | 11.87 | 36.2 | 13.61 | 37.7 | 12.73 | 34.7 | 13.15 |
| Etude 3 (Sight Reading) | 35.6 | 10.11 | 38.8 | 10.75 | 21.2 | 11.09 | 35.6 | 13.10 | 33.1 | 12.92 | 32.9 | 13.22 |
| All Etudes | 110.5 | 29.57 | 118.3 | 30.19 | 69.1 | 33.67 | 107.4 | 40.00 | 104.3 | 39.02 | 101.9 | 38.84 |
| Teacher Ratings | 4.3 | 1.77 | 4.6 | 1.66 | 1.7 | 1.40 | 3.8 | 1.90 | 2.6 | 1.58 | 3.4 | 2.00 |

# Table 23

## Correlations Between Judges' Evaluations of Students' Tape-Recorded Instrumental Music Performances for the Third Year

| | School 1 | School 2 | School 3 | School 4 | School 5 | Total Group | Within-Schools |
|---|---|---|---|---|---|---|---|
| *First Week* | | | | | | | |
| Etude 1 (With Help) | .91 | .91 | .95 | .93 | .95 | .93 | .93 |
| Etude 2 (Without Help) | .90 | .90 | .95 | .91 | .92 | .90 | .91 |
| Etude 3 (Sight Reading) | .89 | .93 | .96 | .87 | .93 | .92 | .91 |
| All Etudes | .94 | .95 | .97 | .92 | .95 | .94 | .94 |
| *Second Week* | | | | | | | |
| Etude 1 (With Help) | .87 | .94 | .95 | .89 | .96 | .92 | .93 |
| Etude 2 (Without Help) | .90 | .89 | .94 | .86 | .92 | .90 | .90 |
| Etude 3 (Sight Reading) | .92 | .88 | .96 | .86 | .92 | .91 | .90 |
| All Etudes | .92 | .94 | .97 | .90 | .96 | .94 | .94 |
| *First and Second Weeks* | | | | | | | |
| All Etudes | .95 | .96 | .97 | .91 | .96 | .95 | .95 |

ability to perform also contributed to the exceedingly high reliability of the repeated performances and the judges' ratings.

## Predictive Validity Results

The third-year validity coefficients, with judges' evaluations of students' tape-recorded performances, teacher ratings of student achievement in instrumental music, and students' composite scores on the musical achievement test as criteria, together with coefficients based on the unweighted Grand Composite of all of these criteria may be found for each of the five schools and for the total group in Appendix E. Corresponding within-schools predictive validity coefficients are given in Table 25.

A comparison of the validity coefficients reported in Table 25 with those reported in Tables 9 (first year) and 17 (second year) show that the predictive validity of the Musical Aptitude Profile over a three-year period is more accurate than the predictive validity for either one-year or two-year periods. The within-schools predictive validity coefficient with the unweighted Grand Composite as criterion demonstrates that approximately

[33]

## Table 24

### Correlations Between Students' Tape-Recorded Instrumental Music Performances on Two Adjacent Weeks for the Third Year

|  | School 1 | School 2 | School 3 | School 4 | School 5 | Total Group | Within-Schools |
|---|---|---|---|---|---|---|---|
| *Judge One* |  |  |  |  |  |  |  |
| Etude 1 (With Help) | .91 | .92 | .92 | .96 | .96 | .95 | .95 |
| Etude 2 (Without Help) | .86 | .90 | .96 | .96 | .93 | .95 | .94 |
| Etude 3 (Sight Reading) | .84 | .93 | .92 | .96 | .92 | .94 | .93 |
| All Etudes | .94 | .95 | .96 | .97 | .97 | .97 | .97 |
| *Judge Two* |  |  |  |  |  |  |  |
| Etude 1 (With Help) | .93 | .92 | .93 | .93 | .95 | .95 | .94 |
| Etude 2 (Without Help) | .92 | .87 | .88 | .93 | .93 | .93 | .91 |
| Etude 3 (Sight Reading) | .91 | .90 | .91 | .92 | .94 | .94 | .92 |
| All Etudes | .95 | .93 | .92 | .97 | .97 | .96 | .96 |

55 per cent of the variance of these success scores in school instrumental music, following a three-year instructional period, can be accounted for by aptitude as measured by the Musical Aptitude Profile prior to the beginning of instruction. The fact that the predictive validity coefficients increased (although at a decreasing rate) over each year of the study suggests that the predictive power of the Musical Aptitude Profile might have been found to be even greater had the longitudinal study been extended over a longer period of time. It is also likely, though not a certainty, that prediction would increase with overall improvement in the evaluative criteria—though it is difficult to conceive of what more could be done to effect such improvement within the practical limitations of a study of this type.

*In this connection, it is interesting to speculate on the possible effect upon Musical Aptitude Profile predictive validity if the teachers could have known their students' initial aptitude scores—thus making it possible for them to adapt instructional procedures more effectively from the very outset of the study.*

The within-schools intercorrelations between the various third-year validity criteria were .77 for all etudes and teacher ratings; .67 for all etudes and the achievement test composite; and .58 for the achievement test composite and teacher ratings. Composite aptitude scores on the third administration of the test (after two years of training) were found to be

[34]

## Table 25

Third-Year Within-Schools Validity Coefficients for the Musical Aptitude Profile as a Predictor of Judges' Evaluations of Instrumental Music, Tape-Recorded Performances, Teacher Ratings, and Musical Achievement Composite Test Scores

| | Melody | Harmony | Tonal Imagery | Tempo | Meter | Rhythm Imagery | Phrasing | Balance | Style | Musical Sensitivity | Composite |
|---|---|---|---|---|---|---|---|---|---|---|---|
| | $T_i$ | $T_2$ | T | $R_1$ | $R_2$ | R | $S_1$ | $S_2$ | $S_3$ | S | C |
| Judges' Ratings | | | | | | | | | | | |
| Etude 1 (With Help) | .43 | .44 | .47 | .40 | .46 | .47 | .35 | .38 | .34 | .47 | .58 |
| Etude 2 (Without Help) | .50 | .56 | .59 | .47 | .54 | .54 | .42 | .47 | .41 | .56 | .70 |
| Etude 3 (Sight Reading) | .47 | .52 | .56 | .49 | .53 | .56 | .42 | .46 | .42 | .57 | .70 |
| All Etudes | .48 | .52 | .55 | .47 | .53 | .54 | .41 | .45 | .40 | .55 | .68 |
| Teacher Ratings | .28 | .30 | .33 | .24 | .24 | .26 | .17 | .21 | .17 | .27 | .35 |
| Achievement Test | .44 | .50 | .54 | .51 | .55 | .58 | .47 | .50 | .50 | .60 | .71 |
| Grand Composite | .50 | .56 | .60 | .52 | .58 | .60 | .47 | .51 | .48 | .62 | .75 |

only negligibly better predictors of success ($r = .77$) than the pretraining composite aptitude scores when the unweighted Grand Composite was used as the criterion.

As high as the predictive validity coefficients were, there seems little doubt but that certain features of this study operated to attenuate them. Such features include the following. (1) Some students were not motivated to make the most of their musical aptitudes. (2) The students were mainly given group instruction and as a result, could not have received optimal individual attention. It is possible, for example, that the extreme heterogeneity of the group in regard to aptitude and achievement forced the teachers to direct their instruction at a level far from optimal for either the poorer or better students. (3) Some of the students enjoyed a much more favorable economic background than others and were given private lessons without regard to their potential to profit from them. (4) Some students may have been assigned instruments in which they were not particularly interested. (5) A few students were allowed, by their teachers, to study different instruments during the course of the investigation and some who took private lessons studied an instrument other than the one assigned for this study. (6) During the course of the study, some students

[35]

experienced physical disabilities (such as normal illnesses, broken arms, tooth malformation requiring braces, etc.) but, nevertheless, continued to participate in the study. (7) Some few students and parents developed rather negative attitudes toward the teacher and the study in general. (8) Some teachers, particularly those who were not involved in the study from the beginning, exhibited poor attitudes toward having to teach students whom they considered less able. (9) In addition to participating in the study, students received instruction in general music which differed considerably in quantity and quality from school to school.

It must be recognized that even if a study of this type could be ideally designed, so that the effects of such attenuating factors might be minimized, a substantial portion of the variance associated with success in school instrumental music would nevertheless be attributed to factors other than musical aptitude. In this study, approximately 50 per cent of the variance associated with success in instrumental music was attributable to such factors. Because the reliabilities of both predictor and criterion variables were very high, it follows that only a small portion of the total variance in success scores can be attributed to such errors of measurement as are usually subsumed under reliability. It appears, then, that to presently unknown degrees, such factors as academic aptitude and achievement, quality and quantity of musical training, interest in and motivation to study instrumental music, physical ability and coordination, and many other factors contribute to something less than half the variance associated with success in music.

It is interesting to note, especially for the purpose of indirectly evaluating the predictive validity and the stability (see Table 31) of the Musical Aptitude Profile composite score, that the within-schools intercorrelations for the various validity criteria over the three-year period were:

|  | Achievement Test Composite | All Etudes | Teacher Ratings |
|---|---|---|---|
| First and Second Years | .79 | .76 | .63 |
| First and Third Years | .69 | .71 | .65 |
| Second and Third Years | .74 | .79 | .66 |

As in the case of the descriptions of the findings of the first and second years of this study, the third-year criterion scores for the 10 per cent highest and the 10 per cent lowest scoring students on the Musical Aptitude Profile were obtained. Composite means for the various criteria for these two groups of students and for the total group are presented in Table 26. As in the case of the second-year results, no overlap whatever was found for these extreme groups on the Grand Composite criteria; the highest Grand Composite score in the low group was 185 and the lowest Grand

[36]

Table 26

Third-Year Composite Mean Scores for the 10 Per Cent Highest and
10 Per Cent Lowest Scoring Students and for the Total Group

|  | Musical Aptitude Profile | All Etudes | Teacher Ratings | Achievement Test | Grand Composite |
|---|---|---|---|---|---|
| Upper 10% | 57.4 | 153.1 | 5.0 | 116.5 | 274.6 |
| Total Group | 46.0 | 102.2 | 3.3 | 88.8 | 194.3 |
| Lower 10% | 33.7 | 55.5 | 2.1 | 57.7 | 115.3 |

Composite score in the high group was 225. This evidence clearly demonstrates that Musical Aptitude Profile scores before training identify those students who will be most and least successful in achievement in instrumental music.

During the third and final year of the study, twenty-three students became increasingly disinterested in learning to play a musical instrument. Their attitude became particularly apparent when they requested that their teachers allow them to take only the minimum required group lessons and that they not be required to participate in any organized band. The wishes of these students were granted. The mean of the initial composite Musical Aptitude Profile scores earned by these students is presented in Table 27 along with the means of their third-year criterion scores. A comparison of corresponding means given in Tables 26 and 27 shows that on the average, the twenty-three students who lost interest in studying instrumental music scored below the overall mean on the aptitude battery and that their achievement score means after the three-year period were far below those of the total group. However, achievement means for these students, except for the teacher rating mean (which undoubtedly reflects the extent to which teacher ratings are influenced by student attitude), were all higher than the corresponding means for the lowest scoring 10 per cent of the students on the Musical Aptitude Profile. This is further evidence that pretraining results on the Musical Aptitude Profile are a more potent factor in determining achievement in music than are some factors other than aptitude. These findings also constitute evidence that there is no one-to-one relationship between aptitude for, and interest in, studying music.

One analysis was made using final-year data which was not made with either first- or second-year data. The criteria which were used to form the unweighted Grand Composite (i.e., raw scores for all performed etudes, teacher ratings, and composite achievement test scores) were converted to standard scores and these standard scores were combined to form a

[37]

## Table 27

Composite Mean Scores for Students Who Took Only Required Work and Did Not Elect to Participate in a Performance Group During the Third Year of the Study

| Musical Aptitude Profile | All Etudes | Teacher Ratings | Achievement Test | Grand Composite |
|---|---|---|---|---|
| 42.5 | 64.1 | 1.3 | 67.1 | 132.5 |

## Table 28

Third-Year Validity Coefficients of Musical Aptitude Profile Composite Scores Using an "Equally" Weighted Grand Composite Score as a Criterion Compared to Unweighted Scores when Used as a Criterion

|  | School 1 | School 2 | School 3 | School 4 | School 5 | Total Group | Within-Schools |
|---|---|---|---|---|---|---|---|
| Weighted Scores | .75 | .70 | .70 | .51 | .68 | .62 | .69 |
| Unweighted Scores | .86 | .81 | .75 | .60 | .79 | .77 | .75 |

"weighted" Grand Composite score.[2] Then the correlation between this weighted Grand Composite and initial Musical Aptitude Profile composite scores were obtained separately for each of the five schools, the total group, and for within-schools. These coefficients, together with the corresponding coefficients for the unweighted Grand Composite, are reported in Table 28.

Although the within-schools correlation between unweighted and equally weighted Grand Composite scores was .96, the difference between the within-schools Musical Aptitude Profile predictive validity coefficients with unweighted and weighted scores as criteria, was statistically significant at the 1 per cent level. The fact that the validity coefficients for the equally weighted criterion composite score were uniformly smaller than those for the unweighted composite is undoubtedly due to the low relationship between aptitude scores and teacher ratings, a phenomenon which was observed consistently throughout the course of the study.[3]

The within-schools correlations between second-year teacher ratings and third-year unweighted and weighted Grand Composite scores are .64 and

---

[2] Each component of this composite had the same variability as the others.

[3] The contribution of teacher ratings to the weighted composite is much more nearly on a par with the other components than in the case of the unweighted composite.

.69 respectively.[4] By comparison, the within-schools correlations between pretraining aptitude test scores and third-year unweighted and weighted Grand Composite scores are .75 and .69 respectively. It is apparent that teachers, in rating the achievement of their students, must be influenced by factors (i.e., attitude, personality, interest, etc.) which, of course, are not considered by judges when rating students' performances of musical etudes.

The possibility that aptitude test scores should be differentially weighted was investigated through the techniques of multiple regression analysis. However, with least squares optimally weighted scores, the predictive validity of the Musical Aptitude Profile was not improved in a statistically significant sense.

In summary, it appears that the Musical Aptitude Profile does indeed function as a valid objective aid in identifying those musically talented students who can profit most from and contribute most to school music activities. In spite of difficulties inherent in the definition and prediction of success in artistic endeavors, the coefficients of predictive validity for the test battery compare favorably to those reported for general academic and vocational predictive tests. Further, because the composite Musical Aptitude Profile score is clearly significantly better for predicting success in music than any single score provided by the test, the administration of the complete battery can serve a dual function; that is, the composite score should be used for identifying musically talented students and, at the same time, the individual subtest scores should prove useful in evaluating students' specific musical strengths and weaknesses for the purpose of adapting instruction to meet their individual needs and abilities.

---

[4] It is important to note that these coefficients are spuriously high inasmuch as teacher ratings contribute directly to both of these composites.

# THE EFFECTS OF PRACTICE AND TRAINING
# ON APTITUDE TEST SCORES

All students who participated in the study were retested on the Musical Aptitude Profile after one and two years of instrumental music training in order to determine what effects practice and training might possibly have on Musical Aptitude Profile test scores. The first readministration of the aptitude test battery took place in October, 1964, and the second in October, 1965.

In order to describe the changes in the aptitude scores from year to year, mean differences (second year minus first, and third year minus first) for the total group of students participating in the study were compared to mean differences found for students who participated in the standardization program (sixth grade minus fifth, and seventh grade minus fifth). That is, mean score differences after one year for students in the study were compared to differences between the corresponding means for representative samples of fifth- and sixth-grade students; and mean differences after two years for students in the study were compared to differences between the corresponding means for representative samples of fifth- and seventh-grade students. These data and the differences between the mean differences are presented in Table 29 for the first-year analysis and in Table 30 for the second-year analysis.

As can be seen from Tables 29 and 30, the differences between the mean differences for students participating in the study (those who received instrumental music instruction) and the corresponding mean differences for students in general (those who were largely musically untrained) were too small to be of any practical consequence. These findings are consistent with those of previous preliminary studies reported in the test Manual.[1] Hence, it appears that formal instruction in instrumental music does not have any appreciable effect upon Musical Aptitude Profile scores. The changes that do occur are most likely a result of general maturation and, to a lesser extent, to the practice effects of retaking the aptitude test and to errors of measurement. It appears that the Musical Aptitude Profile can be administered to all students, without regard to their past musical training or their current musical achievement, and that the school grade

---

[1] Pp. 18-21, 61-62.

## Table 29

A Comparison of the Differences in Standard Score Means Earned by Students Who Received One Year of Intensive Instrumental Music Training With Differences Found in the National Standardization Program of the Test Battery

| | Experimental Group | | | | | Standardization Data | | | | | Difference Between the Differences |
| --- | --- | --- | --- | --- | --- | --- | --- | --- | --- | --- | --- |
| | 1963 | | 1964 | | Mean Difference | Grade 5 | | Grade 6 | | Mean Difference Differences | |
| | Mean | SD | Mean | SD | | Mean | SD | Mean | SD | | |
| T₁: Melody | 46.7 | 9.68 | 50.7 | 10.16 | 4.0 | 47.2 | 9.23 | 48.2 | 9.26 | 1.0 | 3.0 |
| T₂: Harmony | 47.0 | 9.37 | 48.8 | 9.92 | 1.8 | 47.1 | 8.62 | 47.6 | 8.75 | 0.5 | 1.3 |
| T: Tonal Imagery | 46.8 | 8.45 | 49.7 | 9.35 | 2.9 | 47.4 | 7.88 | 48.2 | 8.05 | 0.8 | 2.1 |
| R₁: Tempo | 46.8 | 8.19 | 47.5 | 9.77 | 0.7 | 45.9 | 8.33 | 47.7 | 8.70 | 1.8 | -1.1* |
| R₂: Meter | 45.0 | 8.00 | 45.3 | 9.15 | 0.3 | 45.6 | 8.15 | 47.8 | 8.67 | 2.2 | -1.9* |
| R: Rhythm Imagery | 45.8 | 7.42 | 46.4 | 8.68 | 0.6 | 46.0 | 7.48 | 48.0 | 8.00 | 2.0 | -1.4* |
| S₁: Phrasing | 47.6 | 8.92 | 48.6 | 8.64 | 1.0 | 46.4 | 9.46 | 48.1 | 9.30 | 1.7 | -0.7* |
| S₂: Balance | 46.6 | 9.30 | 47.0 | 8.46 | 0.4 | 46.5 | 8.88 | 47.5 | 9.30 | 1.0 | -0.6* |
| S₃: Style | 45.6 | 8.51 | 47.2 | 8.35 | 1.6 | 46.7 | 8.64 | 47.9 | 8.98 | 1.2 | 0.4 |
| S: Musical Sensitivity | 46.6 | 7.31 | 47.6 | 6.71 | 1.0 | 46.6 | 7.32 | 47.9 | 7.45 | 1.3 | -0.3* |
| C: Composite | 46.4 | 6.40 | 47.9 | 7.10 | 1.5 | 46.7 | 6.37 | 48.0 | 6.72 | 1.3 | 0.2 |

*Indicates a loss for the Experimental Group

[41]

## Table 30

A Comparison of the Differences in Standard Score Means Earned by Students Who Received Two Years of Intensive Instrumental Music Training With Differences Found in the National Standardization Program of the Test Battery

| | Experimental Group | | | | | Standardization Data | | | | | Difference Between the Differences |
| | 1963 | | 1965 | | Mean Difference | Grade 5 | | Grade 7 | | Mean Difference | |
| | Mean | SD | Mean | SD | | Mean | SD | Mean | SD | | |
|---|---|---|---|---|---|---|---|---|---|---|---|
| $T_1$: Melody | 46.7 | 9.68 | 50.8 | 10.64 | 4.1 | 47.2 | 9.23 | 49.5 | 9.69 | 2.3 | 1.8 |
| $T_2$: Harmony | 47.0 | 9.37 | 49.4 | 10.50 | 2.4 | 47.1 | 8.62 | 48.5 | 9.68 | 1.4 | 1.0 |
| T: Tonal Imagery | 46.8 | 8.45 | 50.1 | 10.35 | 3.3 | 47.4 | 7.88 | 49.2 | 8.88 | 1.8 | 1.5 |
| $R_1$: Tempo | 46.8 | 8.19 | 50.2 | 10.81 | 3.4 | 45.9 | 8.83 | 49.3 | 9.36 | 3.4 | 0.0 |
| $R_2$: Meter | 45.0 | 8.00 | 47.2 | 10.25 | 2.2 | 45.6 | 8.15 | 48.4 | 9.04 | 2.8 | -0.6* |
| R: Rhythm Imagery | 45.8 | 7.42 | 48.6 | 9.98 | 2.8 | 46.0 | 7.48 | 49.1 | 8.55 | 3.1 | -0.3* |
| $S_1$: Phrasing | 47.6 | 8.92 | 50.5 | 9.71 | 2.9 | 46.4 | 9.46 | 48.6 | 8.96 | 2.2 | 0.7 |
| $S_2$: Balance | 46.6 | 9.30 | 47.6 | 10.00 | 1.0 | 46.5 | 8.88 | 48.5 | 9.44 | 2.0 | -1.0* |
| $S_3$: Styles | 45.6 | 8.51 | 48.3 | 8.60 | 2.7 | 46.7 | 8.64 | 48.5 | 9.71 | 1.8 | 0.9 |
| S: Musical Sensitivity | 46.6 | 7.31 | 48.8 | 7.81 | 2.2 | 46.6 | 7.32 | 48.5 | 7.66 | 1.9 | 0.3 |
| C: Composite | 46.4 | 6.40 | 49.2 | 8.47 | 2.8 | 46.7 | 6.37 | 48.9 | 7.25 | 2.2 | 0.6 |

*Indicates a loss for the Experimental Group

[42]

## Table 31

Uncorrected and Corrected Within-Schools Correlations Representing the Stability of Musical Aptitude Profile Test Scores After One and Two Years of Music Instruction

|  |  | One Year | Two Years |
|---|---|---|---|
| Tonal Imagery | T | .68 (.83) | .62 (.86) |
| Rhythm Imagery | R | .63 (.84) | .61 (.87) |
| Musical Sensitivity | S | .64 (.86) | .63 (.86) |
| Composite | C | .77 (.92) | .75 (.93) |

norms provided in the test Manual will remain valid. Further, it appears that the test battery can be repeatedly administered to students at different times during their school careers as current needs may demand, and the results of such testings can be validly interpreted from the appropriate school grade norms provided in the test Manual.

The degree to which students maintain their relative standing from year to year on the aptitude test battery was investigated by calculating correlation coefficients between scores made in successive years by students participating in this study. Correlation coefficients between initial Musical Aptitude Profile scores and scores on this same test after one and two years of training are presented in Table 31. All coefficients are within-schools coefficients. It will be noted that when these stability coefficients are corrected for attenuation (given in Table 31 in parentheses), they are of about the same order of magnitude as the reliability coefficients reported in the test Manual.[2] Further, when compared to the intercorrelations of the various validity criteria over the three-year period (see page 36), even the uncorrected stability coefficients reported in Table 31, particularly for the composite score, are noticeably high. It is clear that in spite of concentrated musical instruction over extended time, Musical Aptitude Profile scores display only typical increases; but even more important, students generally retain their same relative position on the test.

---

[2] P. 50.

# THE RELATIONSHIP OF ENVIRONMENTAL FACTORS TO APTITUDE TEST SCORES

The relationships of musical aptitude and achievement test scores to the musical environmental backgrounds of students who participated in the longitudinal predictive validity study were investigated after the second year of instruction. The findings support the hypothesis that such environmental factors bear a *low*, but, in some cases, a significant association with musical aptitude scores. These findings are consistent with those of preliminary investigations reported in the test Manual.[1]

The questionnaire which was completed for every participating student, through individual interviews plus an analysis of school records, is reproduced in Illustration 1. The within-schools correlations coefficients between selected musical environmental factors and achievement and aptitude test scores are given in Table 32. The correlations reported for these scores and the occupation of the head of the household (see Item 21) involve the use of a socio-economic status rating as determined by the occupation of the head of the household according to a system devised by Lloyd W. Warner.[2]

In general, the relationships between environmental characteristics and musical achievement are systematically higher than the relationships between the same environmental characteristics and musical aptitude. Specifically, it can be seen in Table 32 that the educational attainment and occupation of parents, as expected, are more strongly related to musical achievement than to musical aptitude scores although results on both test batteries are significantly correlated with these two environmental factors. Likewise, extra participation in musical activities by students is significantly correlated with performance on the two tests but overall, the relationship is stronger between musical achievement scores and this environmental characteristic than for this same characteristic and aptitude scores.

It is interesting to note that, by and large, aptitude test scores are not significantly correlated with amount of practice but they are significantly correlated with students' attitude toward practice. On the other hand,

---

[1] Pp. 18-23.

[2] Lloyd W. Warner, *et al.*, *Social Class in America* (Chicago: Science Research Associates, 1949).

achievement test scores are significantly correlated with both quality and quantity of practice.

These results, which substantiate preliminary research reported in the test Manual[3]—the effects of practice and training on Musical Aptitude Profile test scores, together with the relationships between musical environmental factors and Musical Aptitude Profile test scores—justify the conclusion that formal background in music, in itself, will not necessarily contribute to the attainment of high aptitude scores; nor will a lack of such background preclude the attainment of high aptitude scores.

Illustration 1

### Interview Questionnaire Employed to Obtain Information Pertaining to Environmental Factors

1. Sex?
   1 Male    2 Female
2. What instrument do you play?
   . . . . . . . . . . . . . . . . . . . . . . . .
   1 Brass    2 Woodwind
3. Do you have a definite place to practice at home?
   1 No    2 Yes
4. Do you practice with a music stand?
   1 No    2 Yes
5. How many days a week do you practice?
   0  1  2  3  4  5  6  7
6. Do you like to practice?
   1 No    2 Sometimes
   3 Very much
7. Do you play your instrument in school other than during lessons?
   1 No    2 Yes
8. Do you play your instrument with other students outside of school?
   1 Never    2 Sometimes    3 Often
9. Did you take lessons on your instrument last summer?
   1 No    2 Yes
10. Do you take private lessons on your instrument outside of school?
    1 No    2 Yes
11. Do you play another instrument?
    . . . . . . . . . . . . . . . . . . . . . . . .
    1 No    2 Yes

12. Do your parents tell you to practice?
    1 Never    2 Sometimes    3 Often
13. Do your parents help you practice?
    1 Never    2 Sometimes    3 Often
14. Does your father sing or play a musical instrument?
    1 No    2 Yes
15. Does your mother sing or play a musical instrument?
    1 No    2 Yes
16. Do your sisters or brothers sing or play a musical instrument?
    1 No    2 Yes
17. Do you have a piano at home?
    1 No    2 Yes
18. Do you have a record player at home?
    1 No    2 Yes
19. Do you listen to music at home?
    1 Never    2 Sometimes    3 Often
20. Do you attend school or community concerts?
    1 Never    2 Sometimes    3 Often
21. What is the head of your household's occupation?
    . . . . . . . . . . . . . . . . . . . . . . . .
22. Did your father attend college?
    1 No    2 Yes
23. Did your mother attend college?
    1 No    2 Yes

--------

[3] Pp. 20-22, 62.

## Table 32

### Within-Schools Correlations Between Musical Aptitude Profile and Music Achievement Test Scores with Environmental Conditions

| Environmental Factors | Musical Aptitude Profile | | | | Musical Achievement Test | | |
|---|---|---|---|---|---|---|---|
| | Tonal Imagery | Rhythm Imagery | Musical Sensitivity | Composite | Melodic, Rhythmic, and Harmonic Recognition Total | Symbolic Understanding | Composite |
| 1. Sex | .08 | .10 | .13 | .12 | .35** | .42** | .39** |
| 2. Instrument | .03 | .01 | .15* | .07 | .21** | .33** | .26** |
| 3. Practice | .15* | .04 | −.01 | .09 | .08 | .04 | .07 |
| 4. Music Stand | .10 | .13 | .18** | .16* | .25** | .30** | .28** |
| 5. Practice Days | .13 | .06 | .14* | .12 | .20** | .25** | .23** |
| 6. Like to Practice | .25** | .18** | .20** | .24** | .35** | .36** | .37** |
| 7. Extra School Activities | .25** | .18** | .24** | .25** | .25** | .22** | .25** |
| 8. Home Music Activities | .15* | .08 | .20** | .17* | .20** | .27** | .23** |
| 9. Summer Lessons | .24** | .24** | .27** | .29** | .28** | .29** | .28** |
| 10. Private Lessons | .03 | .01 | .07 | .04 | .13 | .18** | .15* |
| 11. Play Another Instrument | .18** | .16* | .20** | .19** | .38** | .31** | .38** |
| 12. Parents Tell to Practice | .12 | .03 | .11 | .10 | .03 | .02 | .03 |
| 13. Parents Help Practice | .11 | .06 | .11 | .11 | .11 | .08 | .11 |
| 14. Father Play or Sing | .14* | .10 | .09 | .13 | .17* | .10 | .16* |
| 15. Mother Play or Sing | .17* | .12 | .13 | .17* | .27** | .26** | .28** |
| 16. Siblings Play or Sing | .15* | .03 | .00 | .07 | .17* | .07 | .15* |
| 17. Piano at Home | .18** | .15* | .16* | .17* | .40** | .37** | .41** |
| 18. Record Player at Home | .08 | .09 | .07 | .10 | .15* | .15* | .15* |
| 19. Hear Music at Home | .13 | .08 | .07 | .12 | .24** | .15* | .22** |
| 20. Attend Concerts | .20** | .24** | .25* | .24** | .34** | .32** | .35** |
| 21. Head of Households | .17* | .17* | .15* | .18** | .38** | .30** | .38** |
| 22. Father Attended College | .12 | .17* | .17* | .17* | .35** | .28** | .35** |
| 23. Mother Attended College | .05 | .13 | .15* | .14* | .37** | .32** | .38** |

*r $\geq$ .14 significant at the 5 per cent level

**r $\geq$ .18 significant at the 1 per cent level

# APPENDIX A

Directions Given to Teachers for Rating the Musical
Achievement and Progress of Their Students

1. Put the name of each student and the instrument he plays on one 3x5-inch card.
2. Consider the following rating scale:*

|      |      | Below   |         | Above   |      |           |
|------|------|---------|---------|---------|------|-----------|
| Poor | Fair | Average | Average | Average | Good | Excellent |
| 7    | 6    | 5       | 4       | 3       | 2    | 1         |

Compare each student's musical progress, for the year, to all students you have taught who were also in the beginning stages of instrumental music. Then place each card which bears the name of a student in one of seven piles which represent the above categories. The cards of those students who have made *Excellent* progress should be placed in Pile 1. The cards of those students who have made *Poor* progress should be placed in Pile 7. The cards of those students who have made *Average* progress should be placed in Pile 4. *Good, Above Average, Below Average,* and *Fair* students should be placed in Piles 2, 3, 5, and 6 respectively.

3. Rearrange and check the cards until you are satisfied that you have placed them in the correct pile. Then place the number of the pile that the card is in, next to the student's name. Cards in the *Excellent* pile will receive a 1; those in the *Good* pile a 2; and so on until those in the *Poor* pile receive a 7.

4. After all the cards are numbered, order them into one pile with those marked 1 on top and those marked 7 on bottom. Then put a card on top of the deck and identify the group of students by school, city, teachers, and section if necessary. Put two elastic bands on the deck of cards. Keep the cards in a safe place until arrangements are made to return them to Iowa City. Put all information on a sheet of paper, and retain it in case of loss of cards.

5. If more than one teacher instructed the group, the ratings should repre-

---

*For purposes of correlating teacher ratings with other variables, the numerical value of the assigned ratings were inverted.

sent the collective opinion of all teachers involved. Group discussion is probably the best way to arrive at a single rating for each student after each teacher has evaluated the student independently. The opinion of the teacher who has had the most contact with the students should be given the most consideration.

# APPENDIX B

Form Used by Judges for Evaluating
Students' Tape-Recorded Performance

Year..................

Student Number............... Etude Number...............

Judge....................... Tape.......... Week.............

School........................... Instrument...................

|  | Poor | Fair | Average | Good | Excellent |
|---|---|---|---|---|---|
| Melody | 1 | 2 | 3 | 4 | 5 |
| Rhythm | 1 | 2 | 3 | 4 | 5 |
| Expression | 1 | 2 | 3 | 4 | 5 |

Total...............

Melody: When evaluating the melodic aspect, give particular attention to
intonation.

Rhythm: When evaluating the rhythmic aspect, give particular attention to
consistent tempo, meter, and note duration.

Expression: When evaluating the expressive aspect, give particular attention to phrasing, style, and tone quality.

# APPENDIX C

## ETUDES FOR THE FIRST YEAR

**ETUDE ONE: Prepared With Teacher Help**

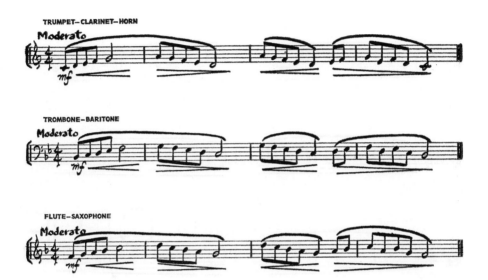

ETUDE THREE: Sight Read

TRUMPET—CLARINET—HORN

TROMBONE—BARITONE

FLUTE—SAXOPHONE

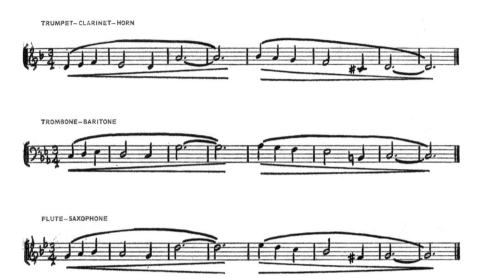

# ETUDES FOR THE SECOND YEAR

### ETUDE ONE: Prepared With Teacher Help

**CORNET—TRUMPET—CLARINET—HORN**

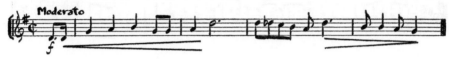

**TROMBONE—BARITONE**

**FLUTE—SAXOPHONE**

ETUDE TWO: Prepared Without Teacher Help

ETUDE THREE: Sight Read

**CORNET—TRUMPET—CLARINET—HORN**

**TROMBONE—BARITONE**

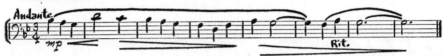

**FLUTE—SAXOPHONE**

# ETUDES FOR THE THIRD YEAR

### ETUDE ONE: Prepared With Teacher Help

**TRUMPET—CORNET—HORN—FLUTE—SAXOPHONE—CLARINET**

**TROMBONE—BARITONE**

TRUMPET—CORNET—HORN—FLUTE—SAXOPHONE—CLARINET

TROMBONE—BARITONE

# APPENDIX D

Individual School First-Year Predictive Validity Coefficients for the Musical Aptitude Profile with Musical Achievement Test Scores as Criteria

## School 1

| | | Melodic Recognition | Rhythmic Recognition | Achievement Test Harmonic Recognition | Symbolic Understanding | Composite |
|---|---|---|---|---|---|---|
| *Aptitude Test* | | | | | | |
| | T₁: Melody | .45 | .12 | .35 | .59 | .53 |
| | T₂: Harmony | .49 | .11 | .60 | .41 | .52 |
| T: | Tonal Imagery | .51 | .13 | .51 | .54 | .47 |
| | R₁: Tempo | .33 | .16 | .11 | .55 | .46 |
| | R₂: Meter | .31 | .09 | .17 | .55 | .41 |
| R: | Rhythm Imagery | .37 | .15 | .16 | .70 | .51 |
| | S₁: Phrasing | .06 | .11 | .23 | .10 | .16 |
| | S₂: Balance | .43 | .26 | .21 | .53 | .50 |
| | S₃: Style | .33 | .23 | .17 | .43 | .41 |
| S: | Musical Sensitivity | .35 | .25 | .25 | .46 | .45 |
| C: | Composite | .51 | .21 | .40 | .67 | .62 |

## School 2

|  |  | | Achievement Test | | | |
|---|---|---|---|---|---|---|
|  |  | Melodic Recognition | Rhythmic Recognition | Harmonic Recognition | Symbolic Understanding | Composite |
| *Aptitude Test* | | | | | | |
|  | $T_1$: Melody | .46 | .54 | .33 | .46 | .58 |
|  | $T_2$: Harmony | .47 | .45 | .36 | .35 | .52 |
| T: | Tonal Imagery | .51 | .54 | .38 | .45 | .61 |
|  | $R_1$: Tempo | .57 | .45 | .30 | .34 | .52 |
|  | $R_2$: Meter | .65 | .40 | .42 | .35 | .59 |
| R: | Rhythm Imagery | .66 | .46 | .39 | .37 | .59 |
|  | $S_1$: Phrasing | .40 | .26 | .27 | .24 | .33 |
|  | $S_2$: Balance | .57 | .50 | .23 | .39 | .55 |
|  | $S_3$: Style | .52 | .47 | .30 | .51 | .60 |
| S: | Musical Sensitivity | .63 | .52 | .33 | .48 | .63 |
| C: | Composite | .70 | .59 | .42 | .50 | .71 |

## School 3

|  |  | | Achievement Test | | | |
|---|---|---|---|---|---|---|
|  |  | Melodic Recognition | Rhythmic Recognition | Harmonic Recognition | Symbolic Understanding | Composite |
| *Aptitude Test* | | | | | | |
|  | $T_1$: Melody | .45 | .14 | .30 | .46 | .42 |
|  | $T_2$: Harmony | .14 | .36 | .40 | .42 | .39 |
| T: | Tonal Imagery | .35 | .27 | .39 | .50 | .36 |
|  | $R_1$: Tempo | .35 | .35 | .36 | .47 | .45 |
|  | $R_2$: Meter | .24 | .26 | .42 | .42 | .35 |
| R: | Rhythm Imagery | .33 | .34 | .43 | .50 | .45 |
|  | $S_1$: Phrasing | −.06 | .24 | −.06 | −.08 | .18 |
|  | $S_2$: Balance | .09 | .34 | .21 | .03 | .18 |
|  | $S_3$: Style | .14 | .41 | .27 | .23 | .38 |
| S: | Musical Sensitivity | .06 | .40 | .16 | .06 | .18 |
| C: | Composite | .31 | .43 | .41 | .44 | .47 |

## School 4

| | | Melodic Recognition | Rhythmic Recognition | Achievement Test<br>Harmonic Recognition | Symbolic Understanding | Composite |
|---|---|---|---|---|---|---|
| *Aptitude Test* | | | | | | |
| | $T_1$: Melody | .30 | .22 | .04 | .24 | .31 |
| | $T_2$: Harmony | .15 | .15 | .19 | .29 | .27 |
| T: | Tonal Imagery | .26 | .21 | .12 | .30 | .33 |
| | $R_1$: Tempo | .18 | .29 | .18 | .45 | .36 |
| | $R_2$: Meter | .37 | .42 | .39 | .45 | .51 |
| R: | Rhythm Imagery | .30 | .38 | .31 | .48 | .47 |
| | $S_1$: Phrasing | .49 | .45 | .15 | .38 | .46 |
| | $S_2$: Balance | .33 | .31 | .18 | .25 | .31 |
| | $S_3$: Style | .27 | .33 | .26 | .32 | .34 |
| S: | Musical Sensitivity | .41 | .41 | .22 | .36 | .42 |
| C: | Composite | .39 | .41 | .27 | .45 | .48 |

## School 5

| | | Melodic Recognition | Rhythmic Recognition | Achievement Test<br>Harmonic Recognition | Symbolic Understanding | Composite |
|---|---|---|---|---|---|---|
| *Aptitude Test* | | | | | | |
| | $T_1$: Melody | .40 | .12 | .42 | .23 | .44 |
| | $T_2$: Harmony | .33 | .13 | .37 | .23 | .43 |
| T: | Tonal Imagery | .42 | .14 | .45 | .27 | .50 |
| | $R_1$: Tempo | .35 | .19 | .37 | .25 | .40 |
| | $R_2$: Meter | .43 | .32 | .40 | .34 | .48 |
| R: | Rhythm Imagery | .43 | .28 | .43 | .33 | .49 |
| | $S_1$: Phrasing | .46 | .28 | .39 | .34 | .46 |
| | $S_2$: Balance | .50 | .41 | .44 | .52 | .65 |
| | $S_3$: Style | .37 | .29 | .38 | .35 | .50 |
| S: | Musical Sensitivity | .57 | .42 | .52 | .52 | .69 |
| C: | Composite | .58 | .34 | .56 | .45 | .67 |

## Total Group First-Year Predictive Validity Coefficients for the Musical Aptitude Profile with Musical Achievement Test Scores as Criteria

|  |  | Achievement Test | | | |
|  |  | Melodic Recognition | Rhythmic Recognition | Harmonic Recognition | Symbolic Understanding | Composite |
|---|---|---|---|---|---|---|
| *Aptitude Test* | | | | | | |
|  | $T_1$: Melody | .48 | .26 | .32 | .40 | .48 |
|  | $T_2$: Harmony | .38 | .29 | .40 | .39 | .49 |
| T: | Tonal Imagery | .45 | .31 | .40 | .43 | .54 |
|  | $R_1$: Tempo | .42 | .34 | .31 | .45 | .49 |
|  | $R_2$: Meter | .47 | .37 | .38 | .45 | .54 |
| R: | Rhythm Imagery | .49 | .39 | .38 | .49 | .56 |
|  | $S_1$: Phrasing | .34 | .30 | .24 | .27 | .35 |
|  | $S_2$: Balance | .41 | .39 | .27 | .38 | .47 |
|  | $S_3$: Style | .39 | .39 | .30 | .42 | .50 |
| S: | Musical Sensitivity | .46 | .44 | .33 | .43 | .54 |
| C: | Composite | .55 | .45 | .43 | .54 | .64 |

## Individual School Second-Year Predictive Validity Coefficients for the Musical Aptitude Profile with Musical Achievement Test Scores as Criteria

### School 1

|  |  | Achievement Test | | | | Composite |
|  |  | Melodic Recognition | Rhythmic Recognition | Harmonic Recognition | Symbolic Understanding | |
|---|---|---|---|---|---|---|
| *Aptitude Test* | | | | | | |
|  | $T_1$: Melody | .50 | .36 | .53 | .53 | .58 |
|  | $T_2$: Harmony | .55 | .37 | .47 | .25 | .48 |
| T: | Tonal Imagery | .57 | .40 | .54 | .41 | .56 |
|  | $R_1$: Tempo | .46 | .38 | .39 | .38 | .48 |
|  | $R_2$: Meter | .57 | .56 | .38 | .44 | .59 |
| R: | Rhythm Imagery | .59 | .55 | .44 | .48 | .62 |
|  | $S_1$: Phrasing | .05 | .17 | .13 | .18 | .14 |
|  | $S_2$: Balance | .68 | .46 | .45 | .44 | .58 |
|  | $S_3$: Style | .50 | .37 | .40 | .35 | .48 |
| S: | Musical Sensitivity | .50 | .43 | .41 | .41 | .51 |
| C: | Composite | .66 | .53 | .56 | .51 | .67 |

## School 2

| | Melodic Recognition | Rhythmic Recognition | Achievement Test Harmonic Recognition | Symbolic Understanding | Composite |
|---|---|---|---|---|---|
| *Aptitude Test* | | | | | |
| $T_1$: Melody | .48 | .44 | .33 | .24 | .43 |
| $T_2$: Harmony | .51 | .51 | .35 | .28 | .48 |
| T: Tonal Imagery | .54 | .52 | .37 | .28 | .49 |
| $R_1$: Tempo | .53 | .34 | .39 | .22 | .43 |
| $R_2$: Meter | .53 | .40 | .39 | .30 | .47 |
| R: Rhythm Imagery | .57 | .41 | .43 | .28 | .49 |
| $S_1$: Phrasing | .42 | .21 | .29 | .16 | .31 |
| $S_2$: Balance | .60 | .38 | .40 | .40 | .52 |
| $S_3$: Style | .56 | .54 | .51 | .49 | .61 |
| S: Musical Sensitivity | .61 | .44 | .49 | .39 | .56 |
| C: Composite | .67 | .54 | .51 | .36 | .60 |

## School 3

| | Melodic Recognition | Rhythmic Recognition | Achievement Test Harmonic Recognition | Symbolic Understanding | Composite |
|---|---|---|---|---|---|
| *Aptitude Test* | | | | | |
| $T_1$: Melody | .54 | .36 | .30 | .28 | .47 |
| $T_2$: Harmony | .34 | .23 | .32 | .21 | .34 |
| T: Tonal Imagery | .42 | .39 | .38 | .33 | .47 |
| $R_1$: Tempo | .45 | .36 | .39 | .35 | .52 |
| $R_2$: Meter | .25 | .15 | .23 | .13 | .24 |
| R: Rhythm Imagery | .38 | .35 | .29 | .21 | .39 |
| $S_1$: Phrasing | −.03 | .23 | .09 | .25 | .18 |
| $S_2$: Balance | .29 | .36 | .39 | .48 | .47 |
| $S_3$: Style | .30 | .23 | .23 | .39 | .37 |
| S: Musical Sensitivity | .25 | .34 | .28 | .46 | .41 |
| C: Composite | .47 | .46 | .43 | .44 | .56 |

[63]

## School 4

|  |  | Melodic Recognition | Rhythmic Recognition | Harmonic Recognition | Symbolic Understanding | Composite |
|---|---|---|---|---|---|---|
|  |  |  | | *Achievement Test* | | |
| *Aptitude Test* | | | | | | |
|  | $T_1$: Melody | .37 | .35 | .21 | .39 | .38 |
|  | $T_2$: Harmony | .23 | .34 | .43 | .34 | .39 |
| T: | Tonal Imagery | .36 | .40 | .37 | .43 | .45 |
|  | $R_1$: Tempo | .19 | .40 | .25 | .31 | .34 |
|  | $R_2$: Meter | .38 | .41 | .45 | .48 | .50 |
| R: | Rhythm Imagery | .31 | .44 | .37 | .43 | .46 |
|  | $S_1$: Phrasing | .49 | .35 | .45 | .44 | .50 |
|  | $S_2$: Balance | .38 | .60 | .51 | .53 | .58 |
|  | $S_3$: Style | .38 | .45 | .53 | .46 | .52 |
| S: | Musical Sensitivity | .47 | .53 | .55 | .56 | .60 |
| C: | Composite | .45 | .54 | .52 | .55 | .59 |

## School 5

|  |  | Melodic Recognition | Rhythmic Recognition | Harmonic Recognition | Symbolic Understanding | Composite |
|---|---|---|---|---|---|---|
|  |  |  | | *Achievement Test* | | |
| *Aptitude Test* | | | | | | |
|  | $T_1$: Melody | .43 | .22 | .14 | .16 | .30 |
|  | $T_2$: Harmony | .31 | .11 | .17 | .23 | .27 |
| T: | Tonal Imagery | .38 | .17 | .13 | .26 | .31 |
|  | $R_1$: Tempo | .41 | .16 | .29 | .35 | .39 |
|  | $R_2$: Meter | .67 | .31 | .42 | .42 | .59 |
| R: | Rhythm Imagery | .59 | .26 | .40 | .43 | .54 |
|  | $S_1$: Phrasing | .43 | .32 | .33 | .48 | .50 |
|  | $S_2$: Balance | .52 | .34 | .38 | .46 | .55 |
|  | $S_3$: Style | .42 | .18 | .31 | .30 | .39 |
| S: | Musical Sensitivity | .61 | .42 | .48 | .59 | .68 |
| C: | Composite | .67 | .36 | .42 | .54 | .64 |

## Total Group Second-Year Predictive Validity Coefficients for the Musical Aptitude Profile with Musical Achievement Test Scores as Criteria

| | | Achievement Test | | | | |
| | | Melodic Recognition | Rhythmic Recognition | Harmonic Recognition | Symbolic Understanding | Composite |
|---|---|---|---|---|---|---|
| *Aptitude Test* | | | | | | |
| | $T_1$: Melody | .46 | .36 | .29 | .31 | .42 |
| | $T_2$: Harmony | .43 | .37 | .38 | .32 | .44 |
| T: | Tonal Imagery | .48 | .42 | .37 | .37 | .48 |
| | $R_1$: Tempo | .45 | .39 | .39 | .38 | .47 |
| | $R_2$: Meter | .51 | .42 | .43 | .42 | .52 |
| R: | Rhythm Imagery | .52 | .44 | .44 | .43 | .54 |
| | $S_1$: Phrasing | .33 | .29 | .32 | .35 | .38 |
| | $S_2$: Balance | .47 | .44 | .41 | .45 | .52 |
| | $S_3$: Style | .47 | .42 | .46 | .46 | .53 |
| S: | Musical Sensitivity | .51 | .47 | .48 | .51 | .57 |
| C: | Composite | .60 | .53 | .52 | .52 | .63 |

## Individual School Third-Year Predictive Validity Coefficients for the Musical Aptitude Profile with Musical Achievement Test Scores as Criteria

### School 1

| | | Achievement Test | | | | |
| | | | | Melodic and | | |
| | | Melodic Recognition | Rhythmic Recognition | Rhythmic Recognition | Harmonic Recognition | Composite |
|---|---|---|---|---|---|---|
| *Aptitude Test* | | | | | | |
| | $T_1$: Melody | .53 | .57 | .61 | .46 | .58 |
| | $T_2$: Harmony | .56 | .51 | .61 | .51 | .59 |
| T: | Tonal Imagery | .58 | .57 | .65 | .52 | .63 |
| | $R_1$: Tempo | .46 | .41 | .49 | .29 | .43 |
| | $R_2$: Meter | .50 | .50 | .56 | .41 | .52 |
| R: | Rhythm Imagery | .55 | .52 | .60 | .40 | .55 |
| | $S_1$: Phrasing | .15 | .29 | .25 | .43 | .34 |
| | $S_2$: Balance | .55 | .50 | .59 | .65 | .64 |
| | $S_3$: Style | .54 | .53 | .59 | .56 | .61 |
| S: | Musical Sensitivity | .55 | .58 | .63 | .72 | .70 |
| C: | Composite | .66 | .65 | .74 | .64 | .73 |

[65]

## School 2

| | Melodic Recognition | Rhythmic Recognition | Achievement Test Melodic and Rhythmic Recognition | Harmonic Recognition | Composite |
|---|---|---|---|---|---|
| *Aptitude Test* | | | | | |
| $T_1$: Melody | .48 | .34 | .44 | .46 | .47 |
| $T_2$: Harmony | .44 | .41 | .46 | .48 | .49 |
| T: Tonal Imagery | .50 | .40 | .49 | .50 | .52 |
| $R_1$: Tempo | .54 | .32 | .46 | .52 | .51 |
| $R_2$: Meter | .50 | .23 | .39 | .42 | .42 |
| R: Rhythm Imagery | .57 | .31 | .47 | .52 | .51 |
| $S_1$: Phrasing | .50 | .25 | .40 | .50 | .46 |
| $S_2$: Balance | .45 | .33 | .42 | .44 | .45 |
| $S_3$: Style | .56 | .58 | .62 | .56 | .63 |
| S: Musical Sensitivity | .51 | .42 | .50 | .56 | .55 |
| C: Composite | .63 | .45 | .59 | .63 | .63 |

## School 3

| | Melodic Recognition | Rhythmic Recognition | Achievement Test Melodic and Rhythmic Recognition | Harmonic Recognition | Composite |
|---|---|---|---|---|---|
| *Aptitude Test* | | | | | |
| $T_1$: Melody | .33 | .45 | .42 | .23 | .36 |
| $T_2$: Harmony | .42 | .45 | .46 | .25 | .40 |
| T: Tonal Imagery | .56 | .63 | .64 | .37 | .56 |
| $R_1$: Tempo | .33 | .41 | .39 | .52 | .47 |
| $R_2$: Meter | .35 | .48 | .45 | .57 | .52 |
| R: Rhythm Imagery | .31 | .47 | .42 | .53 | .49 |
| $S_1$: Phrasing | .37 | .22 | .31 | .21 | .30 |
| $S_2$: Balance | .38 | .47 | .45 | .67 | .55 |
| $S_3$: Style | .45 | .45 | .48 | .48 | .51 |
| S: Musical Sensitivity | .49 | .45 | .50 | .55 | .55 |
| C: Composite | .65 | .71 | .72 | .65 | .74 |

# School 4

| | | Melodic Recognition | Rhythmic Recognition | Achievement Test Melodic and Rhythmic Recognition | Harmonic Recognition | Composite |
|---|---|---|---|---|---|---|
| *Aptitude Test* | | | | | | |
| | $T_1$: Melody | .21 | .46 | .36 | .45 | .43 |
| | $T_2$: Harmony | .38 | .48 | .47 | .53 | .53 |
| T: | Tonal Imagery | .35 | .56 | .49 | .58 | .57 |
| | $R_1$: Tempo | .34 | .36 | .38 | .49 | .46 |
| | $R_2$: Meter | .51 | .49 | .54 | .59 | .61 |
| R: | Rhythm Imagery | .46 | .46 | .50 | .59 | .58 |
| | $S_1$: Phrasing | .69 | .60 | .71 | .46 | .66 |
| | $S_2$: Balance | .55 | .40 | .51 | .34 | .48 |
| | $S_3$: Style | .47 | .35 | .45 | .45 | .49 |
| S: | Musical Sensitivity | .66 | .54 | .65 | .49 | .64 |
| C: | Composite | .64 | .63 | .69 | **.67** | **.74** |

# School 5

| | | Melodic Recognition | Rhythmic Recognition | Achievement Test Melodic and Rhythmic Recognition | Harmonic Recognition | Composite |
|---|---|---|---|---|---|---|
| *Aptitude Test* | | | | | | |
| | $T_1$: Melody | .33 | .32 | .34 | .36 | .40 |
| | $T_2$: Harmony | .49 | .47 | .51 | .48 | .53 |
| T: | Tonal Imagery | .46 | .47 | .49 | .51 | .53 |
| | $R_1$: Tempo | .61 | .48 | .57 | .55 | .60 |
| | $R_2$: Meter | .67 | .59 | .67 | .60 | .68 |
| R: | Rhythm Imagery | .71 | .59 | .69 | .63 | .71 |
| | $S_1$: Phrasing | .47 | .54 | .54 | .50 | .55 |
| | $S_2$: Balance | .53 | .39 | .48 | .42 | .49 |
| | $S_3$: Style | .24 | .41 | .35 | .30 | .35 |
| S: | Musical Sensitivity | .59 | .63 | .64 | .48 | .62 |
| C: | Composite | .74 | .72 | .77 | .69 | .79 |

[67]

## Third-Year Group Predictive Validity Coefficients for the Musical Aptitude Profile with Musical Achievement Test Scores Used as Criteria

| | | | *Achievement Test* | | |
| | Melodic Recognition | Rhythmic Recognition | Melodic and Rhythmic Recognition | Harmonic Recognition | Composite |
| --- | --- | --- | --- | --- | --- |
| *Aptitude Test* | | | | | |
| $T_1$ Melody | .36 | .40 | .41 | .42 | .43 |
| $T_2$: Harmony | .50 | .50 | .54 | .51 | .56 |
| T: Tonal Imagery | .50 | .52 | .55 | .53 | .57 |
| $R_1$: Tempo | .52 | .45 | .52 | .54 | .55 |
| $R_2$: Meter | .55 | .47 | .54 | .54 | .57 |
| R: Rhythm Imagery | .58 | .51 | .58 | .59 | .61 |
| $S_1$: Phrasing | .46 | .41 | .46 | .45 | .48 |
| $S_2$: Balance | .47 | .40 | .47 | .48 | .49 |
| $S_3$: Style | .46 | .49 | .51 | .50 | .53 |
| S: Musical Sensitivity | .56 | .53 | .58 | .57 | .61 |
| C: Composite | .67 | .63 | .70 | .68 | .73 |

# APPENDIX E

First-Year Individual School Validity Coefficients for the Musical Aptitude
Profile as a Predictor of Judges' Evaluations of Instrumental Music
Tape-Recorded Performances, Teacher Ratings, and Musical
Achievement Composite Test Scores

## School 1

|  | Melody $T_1$ | Harmony $T_2$ | Tonal Imagery $T$ | Tempo $R_1$ | Meter $R_2$ | Rhythm Imagery $R$ | Phrasing $S_1$ | Balance $S_2$ | Style $S_3$ | Musical Sensitivity $S$ | Composite $C$ |
|---|---|---|---|---|---|---|---|---|---|---|---|
| Judges' Ratings |  |  |  |  |  |  |  |  |  |  |  |
| Etude 1 (With Help) | .57 | .45 | .55 | .35 | .50 | .49 | .15 | .32 | .21 | .29 | .54 |
| Etude 2 (Without Help) | .52 | .40 | .50 | .34 | .42 | .44 | .18 | .32 | .23 | .27 | .49 |
| Etude 3 (Sight Reading) | .51 | .44 | .51 | .24 | .42 | .39 | .24 | .49 | .31 | .44 | .55 |
| All Etudes | .60 | .48 | .50 | .35 | .48 | .49 | .18 | .42 | .29 | .38 | .59 |
| Teacher Ratings | .28 | .35 | .35 | .20 | .18 | .22 | .16 | .23 | .12 | .17 | .31 |
| Achievement Test | .53 | .52 | .47 | .46 | .41 | .51 | .16 | .50 | .41 | .45 | .62 |
| Grand Composite | .62 | .54 | .62 | .43 | .49 | .54 | .19 | .49 | .36 | .44 | .65 |

## School 2

| | Melody T$_1$ | Harmony T$_2$ | Tonal Imagery T | Tempo R$_1$ | Meter R$_2$ | Rhythm Imagery R | Phrasing S$_1$ | Balance S$_2$ | Style S$_3$ | Musical Sensitivity S | Composite C |
|---|---|---|---|---|---|---|---|---|---|---|---|
| Judges' Ratings | | | | | | | | | | | |
| Etude 1 (With Help) | .44 | .52 | .53 | .48 | .48 | .51 | .30 | .50 | .58 | .59 | .63 |
| Etude 2 (Without Help) | .44 | .53 | .53 | .47 | .52 | .54 | .26 | .51 | .61 | .59 | .64 |
| Etude 3 (Sight Reading) | .44 | .56 | .55 | .45 | .49 | .51 | .24 | .47 | .57 | .55 | .62 |
| All Etudes | .42 | .53 | .52 | .46 | .49 | .51 | .28 | .51 | .61 | .59 | .63 |
| Teacher Ratings | .21 | .35 | .30 | .35 | .35 | .38 | .27 | .43 | .39 | .46 | .44 |
| Achievement Test | .58 | .52 | .61 | .52 | .59 | .59 | .33 | .55 | .60 | .63 | .71 |
| Grand Composite | .50 | .55 | .58 | .50 | .55 | .56 | .31 | .55 | .63 | .63 | .68 |

## School 3

| | Melody T$_1$ | Harmony T$_2$ | Tonal Imagery T | Tempo R$_1$ | Meter R$_2$ | Rhythm Imagery R | Phrasing S$_1$ | Balance S$_2$ | Style S$_3$ | Musical Sensitivity S | Composite C |
|---|---|---|---|---|---|---|---|---|---|---|---|
| Judges' Ratings | | | | | | | | | | | |
| Etude 1 (With Help) | .38 | .10 | .30 | .30 | .25 | .31 | .19 | .23 | .19 | .20 | .35 |
| Etude 2 (Without Help) | .38 | .15 | .32 | .34 | .29 | .35 | .16 | .24 | .16 | .18 | .37 |
| Etude 3 (Sight Reading) | .36 | .20 | .33 | .29 | .30 | .33 | .14 | .26 | .11 | .17 | .35 |
| All Etudes | .39 | .15 | .32 | .32 | .28 | .34 | .17 | .25 | .16 | .19 | .36 |
| Teacher Ratings | .39 | .19 | .34 | .20 | .23 | .23 | .14 | .14 | .19 | .10 | .29 |
| Achievement Test | .42 | .39 | .36 | .45 | .35 | .45 | .18 | .18 | .38 | .18 | .47 |
| Grand Composite | .44 | .23 | .40 | .39 | .33 | .40 | .13 | .25 | .24 | .10 | .43 |

## School 4

| | Melody T$_1$ | Harmony T$_2$ | Imagery T | Tonal Phrasing R$_1$ | Tempo R$_2$ | Meter R | Rhythm Imagery S$_1$ | Balance S$_2$ | Style S$_3$ | Musical Sensitivity S | Composite C |
|---|---|---|---|---|---|---|---|---|---|---|---|
| **Judges' Ratings** | | | | | | | | | | | |
| Etude 1 (With Help) | .26 | .21 | .27 | .31 | .29 | .32 | .48 | .41 | .32 | .47 | .42 |
| Etude 2 (Without Help) | .21 | .20 | .30 | .32 | .34 | .36 | .44 | .53 | .47 | .56 | .49 |
| Etude 3 (Sight Reading) | .33 | .24 | .33 | .28 | .26 | .29 | .45 | .49 | .34 | .49 | .44 |
| All Etudes | .31 | .22 | .31 | .31 | .31 | .33 | .46 | .48 | .38 | .51 | .46 |
| Teacher Ratings | .16 | .14 | .17 | .15 | .15 | .16 | .36 | .33 | .23 | .36 | .28 |
| Achievement Test | .31 | .27 | .33 | .36 | .51 | .47 | .46 | .31 | .34 | .42 | .48 |
| Grand Composite | .33 | .25 | .34 | .35 | .39 | .40 | .50 | .46 | .39 | .52 | .50 |

## School 5

| | Melody T$_1$ | Harmony T$_2$ | Tonal Imagery T | Tempo R$_1$ | Meter R$_2$ | Rhythm Imagery R | Phrasing S$_1$ | Balance S$_2$ | Style S$_3$ | Musical Sensitivity S | Composite C |
|---|---|---|---|---|---|---|---|---|---|---|---|
| **Judges' Ratings** | | | | | | | | | | | |
| Etude 1 (With Help) | .32 | .27 | .37 | .33 | .49 | .46 | .38 | .37 | .42 | .50 | .53 |
| Etude 2 (Without Help) | .37 | .33 | .38 | .42 | .53 | .53 | .38 | .47 | .39 | .53 | .58 |
| Etude 3 (Sight Reading) | .34 | .25 | .37 | .36 | .47 | .46 | .38 | .42 | .51 | .56 | .55 |
| All Etudes | .38 | .30 | .39 | .38 | .52 | .50 | .40 | .43 | .45 | .55 | .57 |
| Teacher Ratings | .23 | .20 | .28 | .33 | .51 | .47 | .28 | .39 | .36 | .44 | .47 |
| Achievement Test | .44 | .43 | .50 | .40 | .48 | .49 | .46 | .65 | .50 | .69 | .67 |
| Grand Composite | .43 | .36 | .46 | .42 | .55 | .54 | .45 | .54 | .51 | .64 | .65 |

## First-Year Total Group Validity Coefficients for the Musical Aptitude Profile as a Predictor of Judges' Evaluations of Instrumental Music Tape-Recorded Performances, Teacher Ratings, and Musical Achievement Composite Test Scores

| | Melody $T_1$ | Harmony $T_2$ | Tonal Imagery $T$ | Tempo $R_1$ | Meter $R_2$ | Rhythm Imagery $R$ | Phrasing $S_1$ | Balance $S_2$ | Style $S_3$ | Musical Sensitivity $S$ | Composite $C$ |
|---|---|---|---|---|---|---|---|---|---|---|---|
| Judges' Ratings | | | | | | | | | | | |
| Etude 1 (With Help) | .37 | .32 | .38 | .40 | .45 | .46 | .31 | .36 | .42 | .44 | .51 |
| Etude 2 (Without Help) | .39 | .34 | .40 | .42 | .47 | .49 | .27 | .42 | .44 | .46 | .53 |
| Etude 3 (Sight Reading) | .39 | .36 | .42 | .39 | .44 | .45 | .29 | .41 | .44 | .46 | .53 |
| All Etudes | .39 | .35 | .41 | .41 | .46 | .48 | .30 | .41 | .44 | .47 | .54 |
| Teacher Ratings | .29 | .31 | .33 | .33 | .36 | .37 | .29 | .33 | .31 | .38 | .43 |
| Achievement Test | .48 | .49 | .54 | .49 | .54 | .56 | .35 | .47 | .50 | .54 | .64 |
| Grand Composite | .45 | .42 | .49 | .47 | .52 | .54 | .34 | .46 | .50 | .53 | .61 |

## Second-Year Individual School Validity Coefficients for the Musical Aptitude Profile as a Predictor of Judges' Evaluations of Instrumental Music Tape-Recorded Performances, Teacher Ratings, and Musical Achievement Composite Test Scores

### School 1

| | Melody $T_1$ | Harmony $T_2$ | Tonal Imagery $T$ | Tempo $R_1$ | Meter $R_2$ | Rhythm Imagery $R$ | Phrasing $S_1$ | Balance $S_2$ | Style $S_3$ | Musical Sensitivity $S$ | Composite $C$ |
|---|---|---|---|---|---|---|---|---|---|---|---|
| Judges' Ratings | | | | | | | | | | | |
| Etude 1 (With Help) | .65 | .68 | .72 | .49 | .57 | .62 | .17 | .61 | .64 | .59 | .79 |
| Etude 2 (Without Help) | .64 | .67 | .72 | .53 | .61 | .67 | .21 | .58 | .57 | .57 | .79 |
| Etude 3 (Sight Reading) | .67 | .65 | .72 | .53 | .54 | .63 | .31 | .56 | .51 | .58 | .78 |
| All Etudes | .67 | .68 | .73 | .53 | .59 | .66 | .24 | .59 | .58 | .59 | .80 |
| Teacher Ratings | .23 | .29 | .30 | .23 | .28 | .31 | .20 | .29 | .33 | .34 | .38 |
| Achievement Test | .58 | .48 | .56 | .48 | .59 | .62 | .14 | .58 | .48 | .51 | .67 |
| Grand Composite | .67 | .63 | .70 | .54 | .62 | .68 | .21 | .63 | .58 | .59 | .79 |

## School 2

| | Melody T$_1$ | Harmony T$_2$ | Tonal Imagery T | Tempo R$_1$ | Meter R$_2$ | Rhythm Imagery R | Phrasing S$_1$ | Balance S$_2$ | Style S$_3$ | Musical Sensitivity S | Composite C |
|---|---|---|---|---|---|---|---|---|---|---|---|
| Judges' Ratings | | | | | | | | | | | |
| Etude 1 (With Help) | .60 | .72 | .72 | .63 | .73 | .76 | .38 | .66 | .70 | .72 | .85 |
| Etude 2 (Without Help) | .57 | .67 | .67 | .65 | .71 | .75 | .32 | .66 | .75 | .72 | .83 |
| Etude 3 (Sight Reading) | .57 | .68 | .68 | .63 | .71 | .74 | .37 | .71 | .75 | .75 | .84 |
| All Etudes | .59 | .70 | .70 | .64 | .73 | .76 | .36 | .68 | .74 | .74 | .85 |
| Teacher Ratings | .09 | .31 | .22 | .21 | .30 | .27 | .03 | .34 | .41 | .38 | .33 |
| Achievement Test | .43 | .48 | .49 | .43 | .47 | .49 | .31 | .52 | .61 | .56 | .60 |
| Grand Composite | .54 | .65 | .65 | .57 | .64 | .67 | .34 | .64 | .73 | .69 | .78 |

## School 3

| | Melody T$_1$ | Harmony T$_2$ | Tonal Imagery T | Tempo R$_1$ | Meter R$_2$ | Rhythm Imagery R | Phrasing S$_1$ | Balance S$_2$ | Style S$_3$ | Musical Sensitivity S | Composite C |
|---|---|---|---|---|---|---|---|---|---|---|---|
| Judges' Ratings | | | | | | | | | | | |
| Etude 1 (With Help) | .40 | .32 | .46 | .31 | .33 | .29 | .21 | .40 | .28 | .36 | .48 |
| Etude 2 (Without Help) | .40 | .34 | .51 | .33 | .35 | .31 | .28 | .43 | .32 | .42 | .54 |
| Etude 3 (Sight Reading) | .37 | .34 | .49 | .34 | .33 | .30 | .33 | .42 | .36 | .46 | .55 |
| All Etudes | .40 | .34 | .49 | .33 | .34 | .30 | .28 | .42 | .32 | .42 | .53 |
| Teacher Ratings | .39 | .25 | .37 | .30 | .18 | .24 | −.01 | .42 | .17 | .23 | .37 |
| Achievement Test | .47 | .34 | .47 | .52 | .24 | .39 | .18 | .47 | .37 | .41 | .56 |
| Grand Composite | .43 | .35 | .50 | .42 | .38 | .38 | .20 | .44 | .34 | .50 | .56 |

## School 4

| Judges' Ratings | Melody T$_1$ | Harmony T$_2$ | Tonal Imagery T | Tempo R$_1$ | Meter R$_2$ | Rhythm Imagery R | Phrasing S$_1$ | Balance S$_2$ | Style S$_3$ | Musical Sensitivity S | Composite C |
|---|---|---|---|---|---|---|---|---|---|---|---|
| Etude 1 (With Help) | .49 | .29 | .48 | .38 | .47 | .45 | .62 | .49 | .48 | .61 | .63 |
| Etude 2 (Without Help) | .48 | .30 | .48 | .47 | .56 | .55 | .65 | .59 | .59 | .71 | .71 |
| Etude 3 (Sight Reading) | .50 | .26 | .47 | .48 | .51 | .52 | .55 | .55 | .52 | .62 | .66 |
| All Etudes | .51 | .29 | .49 | .45 | .53 | .52 | .52 | .55 | .54 | .66 | .68 |
| Teacher Ratings | .19 | .09 | .09 | −.01 | .07 | .04 | .41 | .38 | .16 | .37 | .17 |
| Achievement Test | .38 | .39 | .45 | .34 | .50 | .46 | .50 | .58 | .52 | .60 | .59 |
| Grand Composite | .45 | .31 | .47 | .43 | .53 | .51 | .61 | .60 | .56 | .67 | .67 |

## School 5

| Judges' Ratings | Melody T$_1$ | Harmony T$_2$ | Tonal Imagery T | Tempo R$_1$ | Meter R$_2$ | Rhythm Imagery R | Phrasing S$_1$ | Balance S$_2$ | Style S$_3$ | Musical Sensitivity S | Composite C |
|---|---|---|---|---|---|---|---|---|---|---|---|
| Etude 1 (With Help) | .35 | .29 | .34 | .40 | .66 | .58 | .52 | .47 | .53 | .70 | .66 |
| Etude 2 (Without Help) | .33 | .32 | .38 | .43 | .64 | .59 | .57 | .47 | .54 | .68 | .68 |
| Etude 3 (Sight Reading) | .34 | .34 | .40 | .42 | .65 | .59 | .58 | .47 | .52 | .68 | .68 |
| All Etudes | .34 | .32 | .38 | .42 | .66 | .59 | .56 | .48 | .63 | .70 | .68 |
| Teacher Ratings | .16 | .11 | .19 | .15 | .45 | .32 | .42 | .30 | .41 | .52 | .42 |
| Achievement Test | .30 | .27 | .31 | .39 | .59 | .54 | .50 | .55 | .39 | .68 | .64 |
| Grand Composite | .37 | .33 | .39 | .42 | .66 | .60 | .57 | .52 | .53 | .73 | .70 |

## Second-Year Total Group Validity Coefficients for the Musical Aptitude Profile as a Predictor of Judges' Evaluations of Instrumental Music Tape-Recorded Performances, Teacher Ratings, and Musical Achievement Composite Test Scores

| | Melody $T_1$ | Harmony $T_2$ | Tonal Imagery $T$ | Tempo $R_1$ | Meter $R_2$ | Rhythm Imagery $R$ | Phrasing $S_1$ | Balance $S_2$ | Style $S_3$ | Musical Sensitivity $S$ | Composite $C$ |
|---|---|---|---|---|---|---|---|---|---|---|---|
| **Judges' Ratings** | | | | | | | | | | | |
| Etude 1 (With Help) | .48 | .50 | .55 | .51 | .60 | .60 | .47 | .52 | .58 | .65 | .71 |
| Etude 2 (Without Help) | .48 | .49 | .57 | .54 | .62 | .62 | .49 | .55 | .60 | .67 | .74 |
| Etude 3 (Sight Reading) | .49 | .50 | .57 | .54 | .61 | .62 | .51 | .55 | .59 | .67 | .74 |
| All Etudes | .49 | .50 | .57 | .54 | .62 | .62 | .50 | .54 | .60 | .67 | .74 |
| Teacher Ratings | .27 | .29 | .33 | .28 | .34 | .33 | .32 | .35 | .39 | .44 | .44 |
| Achievement Test | .42 | .44 | .48 | .47 | .52 | .54 | .38 | .52 | .53 | .57 | .63 |
| Grand Composite | .48 | .51 | .57 | .54 | .61 | .62 | .47 | .56 | .60 | .66 | .72 |

## Third-Year Individual School Validity Coefficients for the Musical Aptitude Profile as a Predictor of Judges' Evaluations of Instrumental Music Tape-Recorded Performances, Teacher Ratings, and Musical Achievement Composite Test Scores

### School 1

| | Melody $T_1$ | Harmony $T_2$ | Tonal Imagery $T$ | Tempo $R_1$ | Meter $R_2$ | Rhythm Imagery $R$ | Phrasing $S_1$ | Balance $S_2$ | Style $S_3$ | Musical Sensitivity $S$ | Composite $C$ |
|---|---|---|---|---|---|---|---|---|---|---|---|
| **Judges' Ratings** | | | | | | | | | | | |
| Etude 1 (With Help) | .73 | .75 | .80 | .61 | .60 | .71 | .27 | .57 | .57 | .62 | .85 |
| Etude 2 (Without Help) | .77 | .79 | .84 | .66 | .67 | .77 | .25 | .64 | .61 | .67 | .91 |
| Etude 3 (Sight Reading) | .83 | .83 | .89 | .59 | .66 | .72 | .29 | .67 | .60 | .69 | .93 |
| All Etudes | .79 | .80 | .86 | .63 | .65 | .75 | .28 | .64 | .60 | .67 | .91 |
| Teacher Ratings | .36 | .32 | .35 | .39 | .17 | .33 | .01 | .08 | .29 | .16 | .34 |
| Achievement Test | .58 | .59 | .63 | .43 | .52 | .55 | .34 | .64 | .61 | .70 | .73 |
| Grand Composite | .73 | .75 | .59 | .57 | .62 | .69 | .30 | .64 | .62 | .69 | .86 |

## School 2

| | Melody<br>$T_1$ | Harmony<br>$T_2$ | Tonal Imagery<br>T | Tempo<br>$R_1$ | Meter<br>$R_2$ | Rhythm Imagery<br>R | Phrasing<br>$S_1$ | Balance<br>$S_2$ | Style<br>$S_3$ | Musical Sensitivity<br>S | Composite<br>C |
|---|---|---|---|---|---|---|---|---|---|---|---|
| Judges' Ratings | | | | | | | | | | | |
| Etude 1<br>(With Help) | .62 | .68 | .70 | .67 | .59 | .70 | .46 | .51 | .51 | .59 | .81 |
| Etude 2<br>(Without Help) | .64 | .69 | .71 | .66 | .62 | .71 | .46 | .62 | .59 | .68 | .85 |
| Etude 3<br>(Sight Reading) | .62 | .67 | .60 | .69 | .59 | .70 | .39 | .55 | .59 | .63 | .82 |
| All Etudes | .64 | .69 | .72 | .69 | .61 | .72 | .45 | .57 | .58 | .65 | .84 |
| Teacher Ratings | .33 | .34 | .30 | .20 | .07 | .15 | .01 | .11 | .11 | .15 | .26 |
| Achievement Test | .47 | .49 | .52 | .51 | .42 | .51 | .46 | .45 | .63 | .55 | .63 |
| Grand Composite | .60 | .66 | .68 | .66 | .57 | .68 | .47 | .56 | .64 | .65 | .81 |

## School 3

| | Melody<br>$T_1$ | Harmony<br>$T_2$ | Tonal Imagery<br>T | Tempo<br>$R_1$ | Meter<br>$R_2$ | Rhythm Imagery<br>R | Phrasing<br>$S_1$ | Balance<br>$S_2$ | Style<br>$S_3$ | Musical Sensitivity<br>S | Composite<br>C |
|---|---|---|---|---|---|---|---|---|---|---|---|
| Judges' Ratings | | | | | | | | | | | |
| Etude 1<br>(With Help) | .51 | .50 | .48 | .27 | .33 | .23 | .24 | .37 | .39 | .41 | .53 |
| Etude 2<br>(Without Help) | .39 | .56 | .57 | .30 | .38 | .28 | .31 | .49 | .47 | .51 | .64 |
| Etude 3<br>(Sight Reading) | .38 | .51 | .55 | .36 | .36 | .33 | .28 | .49 | .46 | .49 | .64 |
| All Etudes | .44 | .54 | .55 | .32 | .38 | .29 | .29 | .48 | .47 | .50 | .63 |
| Teacher Ratings | .49 | .40 | .51 | .29 | .30 | .26 | .01 | .50 | .21 | .28 | .48 |
| Achievement Test | .36 | .40 | .56 | .47 | .52 | .49 | .30 | .55 | .51 | .55 | .74 |
| Grand Composite | .46 | .55 | .62 | .42 | .49 | .41 | .32 | .57 | .55 | .58 | .75 |

## School 4

| | Melody $T_1$ | Harmony $T_2$ | Tonal Imagery $T$ | Tempo $R_1$ | Meter $R_2$ | Rhythm Imagery $R$ | Phrasing $S_1$ | Balance $S_2$ | Style $S_3$ | Musical Sensitivity $S$ | Composite $C$ |
|---|---|---|---|---|---|---|---|---|---|---|---|
| **Judges' Ratings** | | | | | | | | | | | |
| Etude 1 (With Help) | .40 | .31 | .44 | .04 | .25 | .15 | .48 | .14 | .07 | .30 | .36 |
| Etude 2 (Without Help) | .39 | .36 | .46 | .12 | .33 | .24 | .51 | .23 | .15 | .37 | .44 |
| Etude 3 (Sight Reading) | .37 | .38 | .45 | .18 | .34 | .28 | .55 | .29 | .14 | .42 | .47 |
| All Etudes | .39 | .35 | .45 | .11 | .31 | .22 | .52 | .22 | .12 | .37 | .43 |
| Teacher Ratings | .33 | .42 | .44 | .02 | .19 | .10 | .37 | .12 | .02 | .20 | .28 |
| Achievement Test | .43 | .53 | .57 | .46 | .61 | .58 | .66 | .48 | .49 | .64 | .74 |
| Grand Composite | .47 | .48 | .57 | .26 | .47 | .39 | .63 | .35 | .27 | .51 | .60 |

## School 5

| | Melody $T_1$ | Harmony $T_2$ | Tonal Imagery $T$ | Tempo $R_1$ | Meter $R_2$ | Rhythm Imagery $R$ | Phrasing $S_1$ | Balance $S_2$ | Style $S_3$ | Musical Sensitivity $S$ | Composite $C$ |
|---|---|---|---|---|---|---|---|---|---|---|---|
| **Judges' Ratings** | | | | | | | | | | | |
| Etude 1 (With Help) | .21 | .25 | .24 | .48 | .55 | .57 | .32 | .43 | .30 | .53 | .55 |
| Etude 2 (Without Help) | .42 | .52 | .52 | .62 | .68 | .71 | .46 | .50 | .37 | .64 | .79 |
| Etude 3 (Sight Reading) | .31 | .36 | .39 | .59 | .67 | .69 | .47 | .45 | .40 | .64 | .72 |
| All Etudes | .32 | .39 | .39 | .59 | .66 | .69 | .43 | .48 | .37 | .63 | .71 |
| Teacher Ratings | .14 | .13 | .17 | .34 | .50 | .45 | .33 | .36 | .30 | .51 | .47 |
| Achievement Test | .40 | .53 | .53 | .60 | .68 | .71 | .55 | .49 | .35 | .62 | .79 |
| Grand Composite | .37 | .46 | .47 | .63 | .71 | .74 | .51 | .51 | .39 | .67 | .79 |

## Third-Year Total Group Validity Coefficients for the Musical Aptitude Profile as a Predictor of Judges' Evaluations of Instrumental Music Tape-Recorded Performances, Teacher Ratings, and Musical Achievement Composite Test Scores

| | Melody | Harmony | Tonal Imagery | Tempo | Meter | Rhythm Imagery | Phrasing | Balance | Style | Musical Sensitivity | Composite |
|---|---|---|---|---|---|---|---|---|---|---|---|
| | $T_1$ | $T_2$ | T | $R_1$ | $R_2$ | R | $S_1$ | $S_2$ | $S_3$ | S | C |
| Judges' Ratings | | | | | | | | | | | |
| Etude 1 (With Help) | .45 | .51 | .52 | .46 | .50 | .52 | .38 | .40 | .40 | .51 | .63 |
| Etude 2 (Without Help) | .52 | .60 | .63 | .51 | .56 | .58 | .42 | .48 | .46 | .58 | .72 |
| Etude 3 (Sight Reading) | .49 | .57 | .61 | .54 | .57 | .60 | .44 | .48 | .48 | .60 | .73 |
| All Etudes | .50 | .58 | .60 | .52 | .56 | .58 | .43 | .47 | .46 | .58 | .72 |
| Teacher Ratings | .30 | .40 | .40 | .34 | .32 | .36 | .25 | .26 | .28 | .36 | .45 |
| Achievement Test | .43 | .56 | .57 | .55 | .57 | .61 | .48 | .49 | .53 | .61 | .73 |
| Grand Composite | .51 | .61 | .64 | .57 | .61 | .64 | .48 | .51 | .53 | .63 | .77 |